DUDE RANCHES
of the
American West

GERRY SEARLE, GRAPEVINE CANYON RANCH

DUDE RANCHES
of the AMERICAN WEST

Text by Naomi Black · Photographed by Will Faller

Designed and produced
by Robert R. Reid and Terry Berger

THE STEPHEN GREENE PRESS
Lexington, Massachusetts

Title page photograph: Lazy L & B Ranch, Wyoming

Editorial assistance: Michael Bingham
Map: Anthony St. Aubyn

PHOTOGRAPHIC ASSISTANCE
AND STYLING
BY COURTIA JAY WORTH

THE STEPHEN GREENE PRESS, INC.

Published by the Penguin Group
Viking Penguin Inc., 40 West 23rd Street, New York, New York 10010, U.S.A.
Penguin Books Ltd, 27 Wrights Lane, London W8 5TZ, England
Penguin Books Australia Ltd, Ringwood, Victoria, Australia
Penguin Books Canada Ltd, 2801 John Street, Markham, Ontario, Canada L3R 1B4
Penguin Books (N.Z.) Ltd, 182-190 Wairau Road, Auckland 10, New Zealand

Penguin Books Ltd, Registered Offices: Harmondsworth, Middlesex, England

First published in 1988 by The Stephen Greene Press, Inc.
Published simultaneously in Canada
Distributed by Viking Penguin Inc.

LIbrary of Congress Cataloging-in-Publication Data

Black, Naomi, 1957–
    Dude ranches of the American West / by Naomi Black ; photographs
by Will Faller.
        p.   cm.
    ISBN 0-8289-0646-7
    1. Dude ranches—West (U.S.)   2. Dude ranches—West (U.S.)—
Directories.   I. Title.
    GV198.96.W47B53   1988   87-29818
    796.5'6'02578—dc19   CIP

A Robert Reid Associates Production

Printed in Hong Kong
by South Sea International Press Ltd.

Set in Baskerville Roman and Hellenic Wide type faces
by Monotype Composition Company, Baltimore

CONTENTS

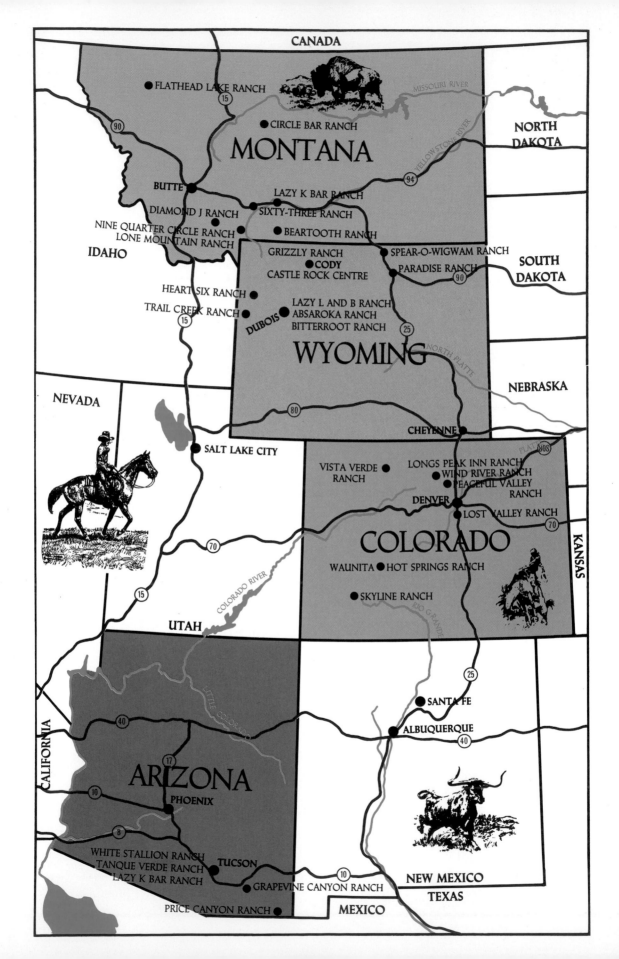

WHITE STALLION RANCH

INTRODUCTION

HOW TO USE THIS BOOK: The text offers a look at the atmosphere and personality of each ranch and its owners. For the more practical information, refer to the annotated directory in the back of the book. Each directory entry contains the ranch address and phone number, who the owners are, when the ranch is open and if a minimum stay is required, rates, and what the guest capacity is. Notes on accommodations, facilities, and activities are also included, along with the elevation, acreage (*see* Acreage and Public Lands), and driving directions. Use these pages, for instance, to sort out which ranches offer laundry facilities or which have swimming pools.

WHAT TO EXPECT: Although every ranch differentiates itself in some way from all others, by their very nature all dude or guest ranches offer similar programs. *All welcome beginners.* Guests can expect to be treated to at least one outdoor steak-fry or hamburger cookout. For this reason, we've omitted "cookouts" from the ranch directory in the back of this book.

A typical riding schedule includes daily morning and afternoon rides that last about one and a half to two and a half hours each. Most, but not all, ranches plan one midweek all-day ride; riders are usually in the saddle for no more than four hours. Many ranches plan their rides according to the desires of their guests; these and a few other ranches may offer more all-day rides throughout the week. Policies change, so if this is an important factor in your choice of a ranch, ask for specifics when you call the ranches. With few exceptions, Sunday is the horses' day off.

Most ranch food is hearty fare: steak, chili, fried or baked chicken, and casseroles accompanied by potatoes and canned or frozen vegetables appear on many tables. Homebaked breads and sumptuous desserts tend to be the rule rather than the exception. When making reservations, be sure to let the ranch know if you have any dietary restrictions. They may require advance notice to accommodate your needs. Most will prepare vegetarian meals, if requested, but if you come from a large city, don't expect a cosmopolitan diversity of fresh produce.

In general, lodgepole pine log cabins house ranch guests. Simple furnishings and western décor predominate. Older ranches often have more twin beds than doubles or queens; the earlier you reserve, the better your chances will be of getting exactly what you want. With exceptions noted in the directory, all cabins have private baths. (This may mean that a family of five is sharing a two- or three-bedroom cabin with one bath.) Some—but not all—offer individual heat and air controls or a wood-burning stove or fireplace.

Water systems, even modern facilities, especially in the desert and at the high altitudes, may need pampering; because of this some ranches may use plain toilet tissue rather than the softest available. Other than that, you'll never notice the difference.

RATES: Unless otherwise noted, rates are per person and include all meals, riding, and entertainment. Overnights generally require a modest additional fee. Gratuities and taxes are extra. Stays of one month or longer usually are discounted. The rates quoted here are for 1988 and are subject to change.

AVERILL'S FLATHEAD LAKE LODGE

RESERVATIONS AND CANCEL-LATIONS: The directory at the back of the book indicates whether a minimum stay is mandatory; often, ranches that require guests to stay for at least one week ask that they arrive on Sunday. At the other ranches, weekly reservations tend to receive priority scheduling.

Reservations policies differ, but most require a deposit equal to the amount of at least one night's stay, which will be returned if a cancellation is made (usually 30 days prior to arrival). Even then, some ranches may take out a small service charge.

ACREAGE AND PUBLIC LANDS: Almost every ranch sits near or adjacent to public lands to which they have access, a factor that extends their riding acreage into the hundreds of thousands. Although the directory at the back of the book lists the acreage of each ranch, do not be misled by small numbers. After each number, the entry includes the name of the forest, mountains, or park that extends the riding range of the ranch. For instance, "Acreage: 180, San Juan Mountains" means that the ranch has 180 deeded acres but has access to public land in the San Juan Mountains.

CLIMATE AND TEMPERATURE: Tucson's sunny seasons generally see days in the mid-60s to high 80s, with nighttime temperatures dropping into the 40s and 50s. Summer, however, is the exception, with 100-degree days. The high desert of Arizona gets a bit chillier, with summer daytime temperatures in the 90s and winter nights plunging into the 30s. The dry air makes the extremes more tolerable than similar temperatures in more humid, coastal areas. Rain, which generally falls most frequently in the summer, rarely lasts for more than an hour. You can often watch storms coming in—or passing over!

Summer is slow to come to the Rocky Mountains. Snow falls year round in the high mountains within sight of some ranches. Even so, days tend to be pleasantly warm and sunny, high 70s in July, with nights in the 40s and 50s. Rain tends to fall in April and May before most ranches open; occasional summer storms usually last for an hour or so in the afternoon.

FLOWERS: Temperature and rain affect the blooming times of flowers, so the following guidelines are approximations.

In the Arizona desert, the ephemeral wildflowers of early spring tend to bloom sometime in March or early April. Perennials such as mesquite, ocotillo, and paloverde bring forth

their blossoms in April and May. Creosotebush flowers, which have been described as snow on the desert, can appear as early as January. The saguaros' white buds open between May and June, while the smaller cactuses—prickly pear, barrel, and cholla—bloom around April and May.

Wildflowers in the Rocky Mountains bloom from early spring to late summer. From Colorado to Montana, you'll see many of the same flowers. Altitude as well as climate affect their flowering time. A general progression of flowers begins with the glacier lilies to wild iris to fields of brilliant dandelions. Next, the blues of larkspur, lupine, and bluebells appear with yellow cinquefoils and arrowleaf balsam. White field chickweed, yarrow and tiny daisies complement the vermilion Indian paintbrush, which becomes common once all remnants of the thaw have passed. Later, the pinkish wild geraniums and vivid purple-blue flax appear with cone flowers, white cow's parsnip, and scarlet monkey flowers.

Although sage is not a flower, the ubiquitous, fragrant plant is found from Arizona to Montana, frequently growing next to some of the flowers mentioned above.

CHILDREN'S PROGRAM: Most children's programs are geared to six to twelve-year olds and include a children's ride with lessons, arts and crafts, and outdoor and indoor games. The more sophisticated agendas may incorporate a separate dining room for the kids, an overnight in a tipi, and/or activities that isolate the children from their parents all day. Most of these programs are optional and allow parents to participate. Policies change from year to year, however, and from season to season. Ask before you book, so you'll know what to expect.

Babysitting services for the under six set and for those children not interested in riding are sometimes not included in the children's program. Where this is so, try to arrange for a babysitter in advance of your arrival; the sitter will usually be a staff member or competent and experienced local person. The service may be con-

VISTA VERDE GUEST RANCH

sidered an extra, in which case parents pay a standard hourly rate directly to the sitter.

LIQUOR POLICIES: Very few ranches have a full liquor license. To accommodate their guests, however, most provide a central gathering place equipped with wet bar, ice, and sometimes even mixers. Cubbyholes and lockers to store personal liquor supplies are often furnished.

SPECIAL EVENTS: For an extra special treat, ask the ranch owners when the fairs and rodeos will be in town. Fourth of July rodeos are most common, but harvest festivals in August and September can be just as much fun.

TELEPHONES: If you can't tear yourself away from office or business and expect to make numerous phone calls, ask the ranch if it can accommodate your needs. Many ranches

LONE MOUNTAIN RANCH

have only one line, which is primarily for *their* business. At others you may encounter a radio phone, which has poor reception or which may not give you the privacy you want. Be prepared to use your credit card or reverse the charges.

FISHING: Fly fishermen are welcomed at every ranch, but not so spin casters. Check beforehand so you don't run into any disappointments. The trend today concerns not only how many you catch, but *how* you catch them, and most ranches encourage a catch-and-release policy, sometimes restricting the number of fish taken per day. While you're asking these questions, make sure to find out whether you will need a state fishing license, and where to obtain one.

WHAT TO BRING: You may be going into backcountry, but you're not traveling deep into the backwoods. So if you forget a toothbrush or decide that you need a different hat, either you can get one in town or you can ask your ranch host to pick one up for you. Keep moderation in mind, though, because some towns, although accessible to the ranches, may be a good hour's drive away. People dress somewhat for dinner, so be prepared to wear something other than blue jeans.

The following list is a compilation based on suggestions from many

ranches. **Essentials:** Cowboy boots or boots with a pronounced heel (not hiking boots); sneakers or walking shoes; two or three pairs of blue jeans; shorts for hot days; cool, long-sleeved shirt to keep the sun off; slicker (not a poncho); brimmed hat; wool shirt or sweater for rafting and brisk nights; sun block; sunglasses; lip balm. **Optional:** Square dance dress; fishing gear; camera and film; hiking boots; lightweight riding gloves; nylons or lightweight-cotton long underwear to protect your legs from chafing under your jeans; bathing suit; insect repellent; field glasses or binoculars; tennis racket; flashlight. If you plan to go on a pack trip or an overnight, request a gear list, because requirements vary. You may or may not have to bring your own sleeping bag.

Of all the items on the list, the one most strongly recommended by ranch owners is cowboy boots. For safety reasons and for comfort on the trail, boots are the best possible footwear while riding. If you wear sneakers or hiking boots, your feet can slip through the stirrups more easily, endangering yourself and your fellow riders. In Arizona, furthermore, boots can protect against cactus spines and rattlesnake bites (if thick enough). Be forewarned: ranches are changing their policies as this book goes to press, and some will no longer allow their guests to ride without cowboy boots.

ARIZONA

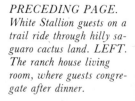

WHITE STALLION RANCH

TUCSON, ARIZONA

Riding and roping in High Chaparral country

A 3,000-acre spread at the foot of the Tucson Mountains, White Stallion embodies the wild west, so much so that the producers of television's *High Chaparral* chose it as a setting for the series. The television cameras are long gone, but you'll still see handsome cowboys. Russell and Michael True grew up on the ranch run by their parents, Allen and Cynthia. The sons, who are now sharing ranch responsibilities, demonstrate rodeo techniques at least once a week, and Russell often leads guests on one of the four daily rides. Fast and slow, on flat land and up in the mountains, the rides offer ample variety for even the most experienced equestrians. The stagecoach stop, a glorified shack that the kids love to play around, has a riding schedule posted on it each day.

Children can't get enough of White

PRECEDING PAGE. White Stallion guests on a trail ride through hilly saguaro cactus land. LEFT. The ranch house living room, where guests congregate after dinner.

Stallion. Peacocks in full feather strut free, roadrunners race by, and an unusual petting zoo is home to pygmy goats, emus, fallow deer, and bighorn sheep. Russell also enjoys introducing the young at heart to Sancho, his Texas longhorn.

A nature walk, guided by biologist Helen Wilson and falconer Bill Girdin, met with great success in 1987. With a surprise up her sleeve, Helen makes the desert come alive. The Trues have an eye for good staff. Their long-time cook prepares a scrumptious Indian oven dinner once a week, sometimes pulling a marvelously moist birthday cake from the depths of the beehive structure. A hayride, steak cookout, and delicious breakfast ride round out the week's activities. Sunday, the horses' day off, provides a break to explore the nearby movie set of Old Tucson and the fascinating Arizona-Sonora Desert Museum.

Nonriders appreciate the Laykold tennis courts, refreshing heated pool, and the redwood hot-tub room. If you cannot or choose not to take a horse, you'll still be able to participate in most of the outdoor meals, whose picnic spots are accessible by four-wheel drive.

Guests who come along often end up

making fast friendships here. Unlike many dude ranches, White Stallion makes a point of welcoming single travelers. It takes only one day to blur the distinctions. By happy hour everyone has met, and Allen, behind his gruff exterior, entertains the gathering with wonderful stories."There are three generations here," exclaimed one single guest who got swept into a card game with a young woman from Switzerland, a mother and daughter from New Jersey, and a sprightly seventy-year-old from Pennsylvania.

Spotless adobe cabins offer guests a choice of accommodations. Many have a living room, and some an outdoor sitting area with cushioned chairs that overlook a cactus garden. The beautiful adobe main house, with an ironweed tree and arbor outside, also has three rooms for guests.

Before your vacation ends, you'll feel as if you've inherited a new extended family. The True's brand of warmth and kindness penetrates even the most difficult language barriers. Guests from all over feel at home here, including the Trues, who first called it home after relocating from Denver in 1965. Twenty years later, says Cynthia True,"I don't think either one of us has been sorry one minute."

LEFT. The Saturday night steak cookout on the patio. BELOW. One of the ranch's free-roaming peacocks displaying his tail feathers.

EFT, above. Naturalist elen Wilson holds up a oved hand on which fal- ner Bill Girdin's trained arris hawk will land. Be- v, a calf roped and tied, ing branded.

ABOVE. Sunrise round up at the corral, set in saguaro country. LEFT. Children, looking much at home astride their mounts, preparing to leave on a ride.

LAZY K BAR RANCH

TUCSON, ARIZONA

The casual atmosphere appeals to children and adults alike

MORE than a ranch, the Lazy K Bar takes pride in its reputation as a "holiday world within itself." This resort attracts families who like the casual atmosphere that allows children to wander into the recreation hall to play a game, perhaps billiards or ping-pong, with manager Carol Moore's ten-year-old son Zane.

Children and adults take part in all the activities, which include a weekly square dance, hayrides pulled by a team of Belgians, breakfast or lunch rides to Saguaro National Monument, and a Saturday night cookout. The mesquite-grilled T-bone steaks taste all the better in the open-air barbecue area under the stars next to a picturesque man-made waterfall. Holidays, too, involve the entire family. Dyeing Easter eggs and a Sunday morning egg hunt have become traditions, as have the rodeos put on during Christmas and Thanksgiving weeks.

To supplement the western diversions,

RIGHT. All guest rooms have private baths and air conditioning.

ABOVE. An afternoon ride heads out behind some of the guest buildings. LEFT. The food served at the ranch, understandably, is heavily influenced by Mexican cuisine.

RIGHT. Guests come ou in the mid-day sun to rela at the pool

Lazy K Bar built two lighted Laykold tennis courts, a lighted volleyball court, and a wonderfully refreshing, flagstone-encircled outdoor spa. The heated pool, well-kept and meticulously clean, maintains a constant 80-degree temperature; it's open all the time, so riders can take advantage of the cool air for a night dip. The head wrangler, rounds out the activities by teaching trap shooting (for an extra fee). And although golfers must leave the premises to pursue their sport, two public and one private course are within fifteen minutes of the ranch.

Most guests choose to ride one of the forty horses, many of which are registered quarterhorses. Rides cover desert landscapes—sage-specked plains, dry washes, and craggy slopes—that may seem familiar. Part of the *Maverick* television series was filmed here, as well as scenes from *How the West Was Won* and the Kris Kristofferson film *Flashpoint*, among others. Carol teaches newcomers how to ride in optional private or group lessons. She's an observant instructor, ever careful about safety and proper riding form. After a session, she may introduce curious guests to Nosey, a pet ferret, a lively creature whose antics invariably draw laughs.

The Van Cleve family of Montana once operated the Lazy K Bar as their winter ranch, but since 1975 Rosemary Blowitz and William Scott have owned the 160-acre spread just outside of Tucson. The mother-and-son team continually update the cabin accommodations, adding new beds, linens, curtains. The result: spacious, contemporary hotel-like rooms with plush wall-to-wall carpeting, individual heat and air controls, and private baths.

The low-slung adobe ranch house dates from 1896, but additions throughout the years have complemented the older structure. Three kinds of bird-of-paradise adorn the exterior walls alongside fragrant cascades of jasmine. The night owls often congregate here, where the wranglers at the Long Horn Bar (BYOB) encourage conversation.

TANQUE VERDE RANCH

TUCSON, ARIZONA

A ranch dedicated to riding— enhanced by modern amenities

TANQUE VERDE'S recipe for a fine ranch blends liberal helpings of luxurious amenities with seasonings of the wild west. While riding is the main activity, two heated pools (one indoor and one outdoor), two saunas, a whirlpool bath, an exercise room, and five Laykold tennis courts hint at the opportunities here. Yet, owner Bob Cote can also tell you of the days when bandits kicked up dust outside the ranch house ramada and when the Butterfield Coach careened by on its way to Tucson.

The ranch history begins in the 1860s. Rafael Carillo set up what was originally a cow camp on a Spanish land grant and registered the R/C brand, which Tanque Verde still uses today. The next owner gradually transformed the cattle ranch into a dude ranch, and then the Cotes embellished the existing facilities, creating a retreat renowned for its casual elegance and impeccable style.

Meals served in the spacious, many-windowed dining room reflect the ranch's ambience. Chef Harland Newton whips up such delicacies as mesquite-broiled duckling with prickly pear cactus syrup and stuffed French toast with Arizona sour orange cream cheese. The results inspire some guests to don skirts, sundresses, or casual jackets for dinner, although just as many could be wearing a fresh pair of jeans and a newly-acquired western shirt. A separate children's dining room gives families the option to eat together or separately during the winter.

Though located only twelve miles east of Tucson, in the foothills of three mountains ranges, the ranch leaves the city far behind. To the east lies the Coronado

LEFT. A typical western saddle, the famous symbol of the western range. RIGHT. The adobe accommodations are arranged around the grounds in small groupings.

National Forest; to the south, the striking Saguaro National Monument.

The wrangler staff greets each visitor at the corrals and introduces them to one of the hundred-odd horses on hand. In addition to daily rides, the lessons, all-day rides, overnights, and cookout or picnic rides form the backbone of ranch activities. Throughout the winter a tennis pro offers his services to guests, and during the winter months a full-time children's program is in swing. The counselor-supervised program is optional, but all children under twelve must ride with the program (parents are welcome to join the kids). The scheduled events—including movies or an occasional bingo game at night—keep most guests busy; for those less inclined to sports and group activities, there are hammocks outside and comfy chairs inside by the card room and main lounge fireplaces. A former bunkhouse dating from cattle ranching days now serves as a bar and meeting place for adults.

At this 58-room ranch, adults and

ABOVE. Children riding confidently through the saguaro. BELOW. The same children are a little less confident on the tennis court, but the instructors will remedy that.

ABOVE. Owner-manager Bob Cote has been cooking flapjacks for years at the outdoor cookouts. BELOW. Dinner is served!—with a choice of three entrées.

children appreciate the tastefully decorated, spacious casitas, most with two queen beds and all with telephone, private bath, and individually controlled heat and air systems. Private patios overlook desert or manicured landscaping that even incorporates labels on the cacti. Kids especially enjoy the birdbaths and javelina feeding areas sited throughout the grounds, another special touch that brings people closer to the desert.

Bob Cote believes that as his guests come to love the desert, they'll keep returning to Tanque Verde. The ranch's bird-banding program also intrigues many visitors. Running throughout the year, the program leaders capture live birds in mist nets, record their vital statistics, and then band them to keep track of their whereabouts. Master birders have banded 154 different species and recognized more than 230 to date.

Tanque Verde caters to couples, to singles, and to families—to anybody who appreciates the flavor of the west enhanced by modern pleasures.

ABOVE. Owners Eve and Gerry Searle (second and third from right) with their capable crew. Gerry, also shown on page 1, is sometimes mistaken for the Marlboro man. LEFT. The solar heated swimming pool is open April through October.

GRAPEVINE CANYON RANCH

PEARCE, ARIZONA

Where remnants of the old west still thrive

RUGGED and wild, Grapevine Canyon lies at the foot of the Dragoon Mountains, in the heart of what was once Apache territory. Remnants of the old west still thrive around this outpost in southeastern Arizona. Eve and Gerry Searle share with their guests a vital, continuing interest in the surroundings, an interest that engenders trips to ghost towns with populations you can count on your fingers, a mining store-turned-museum, a fort on the famous Butterfield Stage Route, and the more well-known towns of Bisbee, Tombstone, and Agua Prieta.

Once Gerry fits riders to one of his ranch horses, they can venture into the rocky mountains dotted with mesquite and Arizona oak, even picking their way into Cochise's Stronghold, the great Indian leader's almost invincible hideout. It's hard not to feel the spirits of the past all around. A few houses have intruded into the primitive scene, but the stream that flows down the rocky slopes of the

RIGHT. Cabins are set back from ranch activities, and offer quiet and panoramic vistas.

granitic canyon may still reveal gold flecks and careful eyes may yet detect an arrowhead.

Guests intent on cowboying can learn a lot from Gerry, and should plan to come in the autumn or in the springtime when the cattle drive is on and all the neighbors join in to help. Gerry followed his brother from Montana to the warmer climes of Arizona, where he earned a reputation as an accomplished cowboy artist and spinner of tales—some tall and some true. But Eve describes Gerry "first and foremost a horseman, then a cowboy and rancher ... There is nothing he doesn't know about a horse." Gerry has even worked as a horse stuntman for *High Chaparral* and in numerous movies, yet when he's passing his knowledge on to beginners, he says, "I'm tough out on the trail. I don't want anybody hurt."

The Searles' horses perform well for their owners. They're taught to work with cattle as well as with dudes, a fact that contributes to Grapevine's policy of lim-

ABOVE. *The Pearce general store is now a museum with artifacts from the Commonwealth Mine, a working blacksmith's shop, and an amusing collection of old movie posters, advertising memorabilia, and turn-of-the-century store goods.* LEFT. *Arizona oak and mesquite dominate the landscape.*

iting guests to adults and children twelve years old and up.

Eve's background adds sophistication to the ranch—especially to the spacious and sun-filled, interestingly decorated accommodations—but otherwise blends in with the all-American style and down-home western hospitality. Eve came to the United States via Czechoslovakia, India, Australia, and Mexico, and when asked will talk of her days as a commercial pilot and flying instructor. Most days, she and Gerry and the crew gather together at the table and in the living room for good, old-fashioned conversation.

Meals will please both meat-and-potato-eaters and diners who hunger after wok-sautéed vegetables. A movie, a swim in the heated pool, a roping lesson, hiking, or a vehicle tour supplement the talking and the riding. Grapevine's intimate appeal reaches out to the guest who rarely ventures from his sunporch as much as to the rider who wants to head deep into lands that still echo their history.

ABOVE. Red rides with a gun and chaps, still standard in the West of the 1980s. RIGHT. Guests and crew eat together ranch-house style.

PRICE CANYON RANCH

DOUGLAS, ARIZONA

A "hands-on" working ranch

UNPRETENTIOUS accommodations add to the atmosphere surrounding this family-oriented working ranch. Owners Alice and Scotty Anderson work their 350 head of Brangus and Texas longhorn cattle throughout the year, so most weeks offer some demonstration of the hard labor that goes into maintaining a cattle ranch. Branding, castrating, inoculating—nothing is modified or changed for the dudes, except perhaps the timing.

January through March finds the An-

LEFT, above. This is the People Barn, and is used for recreation and square dancing. Below, the foothills of the Chiricahua Mountains rise up above the ranch. RIGHT. Wrangler Jayro Manuz plays guitar when he's not tending horses.

dersons packing out feed and other supplements to the pastures. The roundup begins in May and ends when the cattle have moved from high country to low. Summertime brings mending fences and putting out salt. Come October and November, it's roundup time again, when the cattle are readied for market. Scotty makes sure that guests participate as much as they want to—from kids helping to feed the 30-odd horses to adults riding aside the wranglers at roundup time or bringing in calves too young to come in from the range by themselves. Don't be surprised if you find yourself bedding down at 9:30 to be up at dawn for an early adventure.

Scotty's ranch horses, raised on the premises, respond well to riders, especially those who learn under his tutelage. The riding varies with the land, which ranges from sparse, arid grassland to high mountain meadows and stony slopes.

Just as the Dragoon Mountains offered the Apache Indians refuge during time of war, the Chiricahua Mountains, rising above the ranch, sheltered Cochise's people when they were at peace. Although guests feel the influence of Indian history, time here seems to have stopped at a later date, during the heydey of ranching, when nearby Wilcox was the largest cattle shipping point in the nation.

Pack trips (available on request) take guests farther into little-traveled areas, while on-site cookouts and campfires lend

an air of western authenticity that doesn't require venturing into the wilderness. Guests may also be found swimming in the outdoor spring-fed pool and fishing or rowing in the stocked pond. Many choose a peaceful interlude sitting on the weathered dock and looking out over the pastureland with the mountains as a backdrop.

A square dance in the oversized People Barn may take place when the space isn't being used for family reunions or group affairs, such as the annual return of the regional Pony Club, which makes use of the ranch's three-day eventing course.

Normally, however, when guests come to stay they choose from among the airy, newly designed loft room with private bath in the main house; a recently constructed "apartment" with kitchen facilities; a private guest room with a wonderful brass bed and bricked-in walls; and the standard bunkhouse rooms with shared bath.

The main house serves as a central meeting place. Alice's inviting décor uses heirloom quilts and handmade wreaths to cheerily embellish the plain adobe walls, but her creative touch pops up everywhere. One favorite, a wreath made of barbed wire and children's gaily colored cowboy boots, hangs outside the People Barn, where the pool table and "junk shop" draw enthusiastic visitors.

RIGHT. The Buffalo Room, a sunny room in the main house that is a favorite of guests.

LEFT. Owner Scotty Anderson, who teaches riding and will set up a three-day eventing course for experienced riders.
BELOW. Guests often participate in roundups and brandings.

COLORADO

SKYLINE GUEST RANCH

TELLURIDE, COLORADO

Vistas of snow-capped peaks and green meadows

TELLURIDE is literally the end of the road. Surrounded by 12,000- and 14,000-thousand-foot peaks, the village of approximately 2,500 souls lies in a basin of subalpine wonder. Eight miles out of town, on a through road landmarked by the spectacular Lizard Head Pass, is the 180-acre Skyline Guest Ranch, a mountain getaway in a setting that inspired one guest to write, "Our vocabulary has been reduced to superlatives only." Skyline's appeal begins with its vistas, the nearness to snowcapped peaks, mountain lakes, green meadows, and lush wild flowers; but its heart and soul emanate from owners Sherry and Dave Farny. It would be hard to say whether the Farnys enjoy their guests more than the outdoors; they love both so much.

Dave ran the Aspen Highlands Ski School and directed the Telluride Mountaineering School, where leadership skills were stressed more than the competitiveness often associated with sporting activities. He hoped that the participants would leave with a passion for nature. This philosophy embodies time spent at Skyline and elevates it from a simple vacation into an experience that will be indelibly marked on your memory.

Guests can ride horses along simple trails by the rough-barked Engelmann spruce lodge or up into the mountains to an old miner's cabin, to aspen woods where elk are often seen, and to rushing falls. For a change of pace many of the same destinations are within walking dis-

tance. Dave provides a pick-up service so hikers can journey in one direction without having to backtrack. In a concise, useful pamphlet, Dave and Sherry describe the hikes, climbs, and pathways, rating them so hikers have a better chance of finding the right outing to suit individual needs. For those guests with experience, Dave will share his knowledge of technical climbing. Visitors may also take advantage of jeep trips, river rafting, and sightseeing excursions to Mesa Verde, one of the country's most striking preserves of Indian cliff dwellings.

After a day of hot and dusty touring,

PRECEDING PAGES. ...apped mountains in ...June, near Skyline ... LEFT. The main ...house, made of Engel-...spruce logs. RIGHT. ...gler Paul Finley, ...wife is also a wran-

Owners Dave and Sherry Farny.

peaks. On Monday the wranglers check out the guests' riding abilities and give lessons, if desired, while nonriders can opt for fly fishing instruction. For the better part of the week, guests choose their passion which might even be river rafting or kayaking. Pack a lunch, and you're off; or you can plan to partake of the midday buffet and relax until the sun sets. The breakfast ride on Friday leads to the base of the Ophir Needles, an unusual rock formation. Friday is also town day. Some hikers leave from town to explore the hills that slope up from the end of the main street.

Many guests eagerly look forward to the Farnys' Saturday Spectaculars, all-day trips that take riders farther into the backcountry and that much closer to what they fondly refer to as "the mountain joy." If that doesn't get you to relax, a few minutes in the sauna or under the stars in the wood-burning hot tub should do the trick.

the ranch's two lakes look refreshingly inviting. Toward nightfall fly fishermen replace swimmers. "It is not uncommon for a guest to catch two- to three-pound trout," Dave says. Stocked Tasmanian rainbows share the upper pond with native browns and rainbows. Although this satisfies most guests, serious anglers can venture to higher waters where swift and clear streams practically give away cutthroat trout.

As with most of Colorado's dude ranches, Skyline hosts people from Sunday to Sunday with a planned program that revolves around each guest's expectations, combining the best properties of organization and flexibility. Sundays are get-acquainted days, with a campfire cookout in the meadow below the lodge, right in sight of Mt. Wilson, El Diente, and Wilson Peak, all 14,000-plus-foot

RIGHT, above. Dave Farny, at daybreak, casting for one of the 4,000 trout stocked in the Upper Lake. Below, Paul Finley herding horses down to the ranch from the winter range.

BELOW. The wood-fired, outdoor hot tub feels like a million dollars. Other guests enjoy nearby white water kiyacking.

WAUNITA HOT SPRINGS RANCH

GUNNISON, COLORADO

Where good humor and music abound

THE warmth from Waunita Hot Springs radiates from the Pringle family as much as from the renowned 175-degree natural springs by the side of the historic ranch house. Although the water may cool to a temperate 90 degrees in the 35-by-90-foot swimming pool, the hospitality of the three generations of hosts is always warm.

Family and personality play a large role in the activities at Waunita: good humor and music abound. Rod and Junelle, the elders of the bunch, moved from Houston where Rod worked as an athletic director for the YMCA. Sons Wes and Ryan, both small children at the time of the relocation, now help run the ranch with their wives. In one guise Wes, as Mr. Wizard, will amaze his guests by boiling water in a paper cup over a raging

LEFT. The blend of campfire smoke in a scented pine grove is unforgettable. RIGHT. The Pringle family portrait (from left to right): Brody, Wes, Kari, Junelle, Jessica, Rod, Ryan, Tammy.

fry also love the petting farm, where they can help gather eggs and feed the goats. Everyone enjoys the overnight and float trip included in the week's activities. Most days, however, center around the 55 head of well-trained horses and scenic trail rides. Nonriders take note: All of the cookouts are accessible by four-wheel drive.

Elk calve in the lower woods in June, treating some early summer visitors to a glimpse of these regal animals before they retreat to the high country. Lodgepole pines predominate with clusters of Ponderosa pine and aspen, so most of the riding is at a gentle pace.

Whether you ride or not, you'll still be struck by the sincerity, simplicity, and harmony here that add up to a refreshing, robust vacation.

campfire. In another, he teams up with his wife Kari, Ryan, his sister-in-law Tammy, and neighbor Jim Harris to perform a professional roundup of western, cowboy, and love songs. They are extraordinarily good, and the good times they're having on stage infect the audience.

Wes, who is getting his masters degree in botany, has set up an experimental greenhouse using the water from the hot springs, where he grows strawberries, cucumbers, and tomatoes for the ranch. The unpretentious food is good and filling fare, served family or buffet style after a brief blessing. In-between meals, guests heed the no-alcohol policy and help themselves to iced tea, lemonade, fresh fruit, and cookies, another hallmark of Waunita's simple charm.

"The ranch is at 8,946 feet," says Junelle. "By the time you get upstairs, 9,000." Only ten miles from the Continental Divide and twenty-seven miles from Gunnison, Waunita Hot Radium Springs, as it was originally called, began as a health spa at the turn of the century. Today guests lodge in tidy, hotel-style rooms with simple wood furnishings and spotless modern bathrooms.

Tomichi Dome serves as a backdrop to the 121-acre ranch. The mountainous bulge is an omnipresent reminder of the fertile Indian history that gave Waunita its name and that still yields occasional arrowheads. Junelle takes the kids up to a nearby slope and shows them where to hunt for arrowhead chips as part of an Indian breakfast treasure hunt. The small-

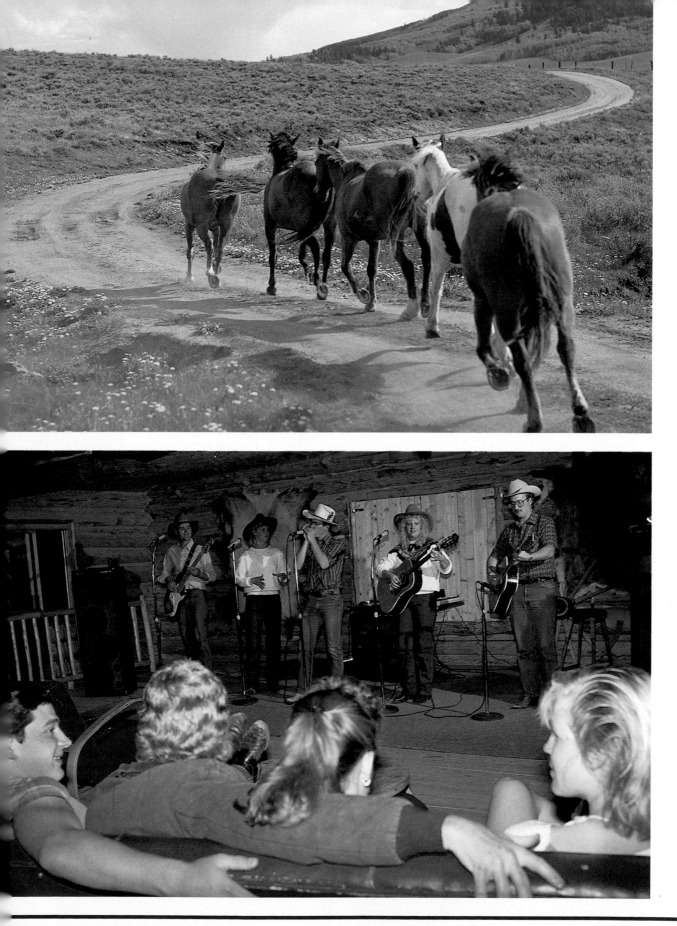

LOST VALLEY RANCH

DECKERS, COLORADO

Wholesome, well-organized family fun

FROM the moment the wrangler on horseback greets visitors at the gate and asks, "You lookin' for Lost Valley Ranch?" a relaxed atmosphere prevails. After assuring that, "You're in the right place," the mounted bellhop leads arrivals to Bob Foster Jr., who snaps a Polaroid picture of each incoming group to put on the Family Album bulletin board.

Lost Valley packs the days with activities. "We provide a complete program, but our guests can take it or leave it," says Bob Jr. The Sunday-to-Sunday schedule begins with a colorful poolside spaghetti luncheon and ends the following week with a peaceful morning worship service at the pastoral Chapel in the Pines. In-between there are after-dinner musicals performed by the staff, a wranglers' rodeo complete with national anthem and bucking broncos, a square dance, a Hay Loft Opera House Melodrama, and a night to put the family brand on the dining hall walls, a tradition

that guests continue each year they come by putting a checkmark next to their initial brand.

A strong children's program for six to twelve-year-olds helps set Lost Valley apart. Parents can and do drop off their kids with the counselors and meet them for dinner; even then, many of the older children choose to eat with each other. As the brochure states, "Your only chore will be to get them to bed each night." Toddlers from three to five play under supervision while mom and dad ride; babies two and under, however, are the responsibility of their parents.

Lost Valley outdoes itself offering wholesome, well-organized family fun. Approximately half of the fifty-two staff

Marion and Bob Foster Sr.

members came as guests before signing on for the summer. Clean-cut, outgoing, and very all-American, the crew works hard to make every guest feel special; and with a roughly two-to-one guest-to-staff ratio, that's not hard to do.

The Fosters place a premium on comfort for their guests. Half of the twenty-four one-to three-bedroom cabin suites are single-family structures with living room, oversized queen or king beds, Louis L'Amour paperbacks on the fireplace mantels, and wall-to-wall carpeting.

Lost Valley, which sits at 7,000 feet on the eastern slope of the mountains, was once a secluded fishing camp. The Fosters believe that their isolated location, at the end of a beautiful, wooded nine-mile dirt road, necessitates their emphasis on Rocky Mountain luxury.

The senior Robert Fosters took over the ranch in 1960, expanding and adding hot tubs, swimming pool, and tennis courts. They do have cattle here, but if you want a working ranch vacation, schedule to come for the spring round-up.

Although the Fosters came from a business background, they've taken to ranching with ease. "Like so many things, you learn by doing," says Bob Sr. The handsome horses stand as living proof to this statement. Riders team up with others of their ability, so while one group may scale a ridge and lope along the high meadows, another will leisurely climb up to a rocky overlook for the stunning view.

RIGHT. The ranch pu
its own rodeos.
BELOW. Guests grill
own steaks at the Satur
night cookouts. Interiors
rustically modern.

LONGS PEAK INN AND GUEST RANCH

LONGS PEAK INN AND GUEST RANCH

ESTES PARK, COLORADO

Ride one of sixty sure-footed mountain horses

A 1904 advertisement hanging on the dining room wall enticed visitors to the Longs Peak Inn eleven years before neighboring Rocky Mountain National Park became an officially designated tourist attraction: Its words still ring true:

Near snowy peaks where poetic trails begin . . . the most artistically rustic inn in America. . . . on the heights, amid the peaks of the Rockies close to perpetual snow and strange timberline . . . nearer the sky than any hotel in Europe.

Although the ranch relinquished some of its rusticity for comfort when former owners refurbished the interiors and added Alpine-style white stucco and dark wood trim to the log cabins, the Swiss village buildings stand in whimsical contrast to the exquisitely crafted original log lodge and cabins that now house the staff. With one exception, guests stay in the more modern buildings to take advantage of their spaciousness and contemporary, clean facilities. Those who hanker after

T, above. Wranglers, indispensable on a , especially to guests, find out most of what need to know from . Below, wranglers and s leaving for a ride. g to 14,256 feet, just e right out of the photo, ngs Peak.

RIGHT. The Swiss-style ranch house incorporates the dining room, recreation hall, living room, and office under one roof.

afternoon rainstorms). On the other side of the ranch, just across Route 7, Twin Sisters rises up, tempting less zealous day-hikers to its 11,428-foot summit.

For guests who would rather trust the ups and downs to a four-footed creature, Longs Peak Inn stables sixty sure-footed mountain horses who, under the care of safety-conscious wranglers, transport even the smallest six-year-old happily. Children love Longs Peak Inn: the counselor works in conjunction with the children's wrangler to provide a full days' worth of activity. Many parents opt to join in the fun, riding or swimming with their children or helping out with a scavenger hunt or an arts-and-crafts project.

The Akins gear even the nightime pro-

LEFT. A fire in the living room for chilly mountain evenings; chuckwagon bread, made in coffee cans; the heated pool adjacent to the ranch house.

more traditional housing can request Grizzly, a wonderfully countrified log hideaway tucked into the trees within a stone's throw of one of the five stocked ponds on Bob and Virginia Akins' 250-acre ranch.

Longs Peak, at 14,256 feet, the tallest mountain in the park, towers above the mostly wooded acreage. It's an arduous 12-hour climb for trekkers willing to start out at 2 or 3 in the morning (to miss the

ABOVE. Longs Peak and Wind River share cookout sites. The breakfast ride ends here at Longs Peak, the dinner ride at Wind River.

grams to families. The 1987 roster incorporated into the schedule a weekly square dance, barbecue cookout, bingo, nature talk, and ice cream social. Overall, the varied program is the ranch's strongest feature. With morning, afternoon, and occasional all-day rides geared to the varying abilities of visitors, Bob and Virginia also plan vehicle tours of the national park and outlying areas, lowland hikes to satisfy bird- and waterfall-watchers, beginners' rafting trips on the Colorado River, and an overnight trail ride for adults and children over twelve. Children from 6 to 11 have their own over-

night campout complete with teepees. There's even a wine-and-cheese ride "for the old softies," says Bob. "And fishing."

Before buying the ranch, Bob and Virginia owned restaurant franchises in northern Colorado, and they bring their culinary expertise to the dining room where, at tables for two, four, or more, guests can choose an entrée and sip a cocktail with dinner or, later, in the upstairs lounge.

Nights wind down with guests and staff mixing around one of the main house's two stone fireplaces or playing pool or ping-pong in the recreation room.

WIND RIVER RANCH

ESTES PARK, COLORADO

Where activities match the peerless facilities

SET BACK from the road and tucked into the peaks surrounding Rocky Mountain National Park, Wind River Ranch showcases the very best of Colorado's beauty. "The National Park is our back boundary," says Rob Irvin, who, with his wife Jere, takes the most active role in running the ranch. Radiating charm and sophistication, the Irvin family sees to it that everything within sight pleases the eye, from the grassy horse paddock to the splendidly situated rock-walled pool to the stained-glass adorned dining room.

Collections and knickknacks fill the walls and spaces of the dining room, creating an atmosphere that complements the delicious food. A lovely Victorian inkwell sits among the array of old glass on the windowsills; an assortment of blue-and-white Jule plates flatters the golden hue of the wood walls; and an unusual assembly of outmoded shoe lasts

ABOVE. The Irvin's sweet-smelling barn and corral, standing in full view of the peaks of Rocky Mountain National Park. LEFT. Everyone uses the pool for lounging, whether they swim or not.

Rob and Jere Irvin, who met at the ranch.

ABOVE. Wranglers pose
the back of the wonderful
barn.

and irons stand as counterpoint to the
attractive Indian rugs hanging on either
side of the paned picture window.

The twenty-eight guest cabins and
rooms follow through with a similar sense
of design. Antiques blend in with Indian
crafts and more traditional ranch appointments, with a stone fireplace or
woodstove found in some rooms. For
instance, Miss Bondi's Room, which honors actress and former guest Buelah Bondi,
features a wonderful Victorian bed, green
wicker furniture, and a small porch. Another chamber, awash in soft blues, sports
framed turn-of-the-century valentines on
the walls and quilts on the twin beds;
another, in tawny earth tones, highlights
a tasteful chintz chair, antique secretary,
and subtly colored bird prints. Each room
has its own special charm, and all offer
individually controlled heat, carpeting,
and private bath.

The activities match the peerless facilities: horseback riding offered by the hour,
day, or week; breakfast and lunch rides;
whitewater rafting on the Colorado (extra
fee); and an old-time country-western
campfire. Nighttime amusements also include a talk by a local naturalist, bingo,
movies, and happy hours on Rob and

Jere's porch (watch for buzzing hummingbirds). Thursday night is Hat Night: "If you expect to be served dinner, you have to have wearing apparel on your head," says Rob, so guests come to happy hour wearing crazy, creative headgear. Don't blame the Irvins; the tradition began with a fun-loving group of guests who kept meeting up with each other at the ranch year after year. The idea prompted such good times that the Irvins adopted it as a weekly ritual.

A children's counselor takes care of the youngsters, leading them around the corral on one of the ranch's well-trained horses or watching over them at the playground. The recreation hall draws the younger set, too. Adults tend to gather at the whirlpool spa, which will work out any kinks brought on by hard riding or touring. Just a walk can clear the head immeasurably; at 9,200 feet the air is clean, the mountains close, and at night the stars seem only an arm's reach away.

RIGHT. One of the two guest cabins with stone fireplaces.

An artist sketching by the St. Vrain River, which runs through the property past the ranch houses.

PEACEFUL VALLEY LODGE AND GUEST RANCH

LYONS, COLORADO

A European village bustling with western activity

PEACEFUL VALLEY is hardly a typical guest ranch. Austrian-style wood-frame chalets sport bright red-and-white shutters and turquoise gingerbread trim. The requisite log cabins recall homestead days, but the overall feeling here remains one of a European village bustling with western activity.

Owner Karl Boehm left his native Austria in circumstances similar to the famous von Trapp family. Once settled in Kentucky he met his future wife Mabel "and that started a whole new adventure," recalls Karl. "After Pearl Harbor, I wanted to do my part," he says. So this strong-willed, soft-spoken patriarch enlisted as one of the original Tenth Mountaineers—the first military division to train and fight on skis in mountain combat. After serving as an investigator in the Nuremberg trials, receiving his masters in international relations from

Georgetown University, and spending a number of years with the State Department, Karl came to Colorado looking for a place to settle. On his second day he discovered Peaceful Valley.

"The day after we moved our furniture in, the whole place burned down . . . we started from scratch." That gave the Boehms a chance to modernize. Today's accommodations range from pine-paneled and carpeted lodge rooms to cabins with kitchenette, fireplace, and living room to deluxe hotel-style rooms with king-size bed, bathtub whirlpool, refrigerator, and telephone.

From the room options to the indoor heated swimming pool, Peaceful Valley's details emerged from the seeds of Karl and Mabel Boehm's original vision. "Whatever we try to do, we do the best we can," says Karl, recounting a visit of the Korean representative from the 1988 Olympics, who came to look at the ranch

ABOVE. Peaceful Valley was once a village with its own post office. RIGHT. Presiding over the Saturday night buffet table are (from left to right) Randy Eubank, Grandmother Boehm, Mabel Boehm and staff.

pool's unique heating and purification system.

The trend toward quality also shows up in the corral. Head wrangler Charlie Cox worked as a jockey for 14 years. He demands a lot from his staff, requiring a videotape of them in action before he hires them. "We're interested in people who are horsemen, not cowboys," explains Charlie. Observant guests may notice the two dozen or so Lippizaner-Arabian bred horses. The mix, inadvert-

ently masterminded by Karl, captures the best of both types of horse, producing an animal noted for its responsiveness, endurance, and even temper.

All guests, even experienced riders, must be checked out in either the outdoor or indoor arenas. Once that's done, Charlie offers rides to suit whatever the group wants, organizing teens and children's rides, too, if there's enough interest. Hearty equestrians can sign up for all-day or overnight rides.

Peaceful Valley also accommodates nonriders, with van trips along a scary but stunning former narrow-gauge railroad corridor, over the pass in Rocky Mountain National Park, and to scenic overlooks for picnics by glacial lakes. Filling out the ranch's programs are square dances, a costume party and talent show, kaffee klatsches, poolside barbecues, and hayrides.

Daughter Debbie and son-in-law Randy, both warm, easy-going hosts, plan to continue the Boehm family tradition, a tradition that draws its inspiration from the mountains only a few minutes' ride away.

ABOVE. *Head wrangler*
Charlie Cox and other
wranglers, photographed in
the horse barn. LEFT. *The*
breakfast ride features
songs, URF's (Uncle Ran-
dy's Famous hashbrowns),
and tossed omelets.

The solar heated, indoor
swimming pool is of Olym-
pic proportions.

VISTA VERDE GUEST RANCH

STEAMBOAT SPRINGS, COLORADO

An opportunity to explore superb countryside

ONCE a week, early in the morning, guests clamber on to a 1943 red firetruck with schoolhouse seats and, wrapping themselves in warm sweaters, set out to meet one of the largest hot-air balloons in the world. After the billowing 3,000 square yards of fabric are inflated and the balloon towers 100 feet tall, the guests climb in for what the pilot calls "a floating nature walk." Following the main canyon of the Elk River, the rainbow-colored airbag dips into the trees for its passengers to collect pinecones, then soars to higher altitudes for views of three states. "I saw about forty deer, two elk, and a few hummingbirds," recalled one guest. She had just finished her champagne-enhanced indoctrination into the hot air balloon society.

The balloon brings an added dimension to this already sophisticated vacation. Frank and Winton Brophy, transplanted easterners from Westchester County, New York, maintain a casual western ambience but spare their guests no comfort. Their chef hails from the

Owners Winton and Frank Brophy with a recent acquisition, a 1929 Ford Model A roadster.

renowned Culinary Institute of America, a masseuse is on-call, and the redwood-decked, plant-filled spa lures waist-watchers with an exercise bicycle, rowing machine, wet sauna, and whirlpool. White water rafting on the challenging upper Colorado River, with licensed guides, is well suited to families.

Yet, these extras only supplement the riding and relaxing that take center stage here. Unlike many Rocky Mountain hideaways, Vista Verde—at the end of a six-

LEFT. About 90 per cent of the guests opt for a hot air balloon ride in the cool, early morning air. BELOW. This three bedroom log cabin has a wood stove and calico curtains, a ranch trademark.

ettes. Hand-hewn pine or spruce furniture complements calico curtains and hooked rugs, a design scheme that's partly carried over into the main lodge library.

The rest of the tastefully decorated main ranch building reflects the owners' love of antiques, many of which traveled west with the Brophys. The handsome array of pewter on the mantel "came from a big collection of attics on both sides of the family," says Winton. Glass bottles—new and old, small and large, clear and colored—bring the windowsills to life when the sun shines in just the right way. And, as you serve yourself coffee or tea, take note of the white Monarch stove that does double duty as a countertop.

The understated elegance appeals to adults and children alike. Kids will love the two wooden Indians that stand guard in a windowed alcove by one dining room table. They'll also delight in Fort Smiles, a wooden treehouse fort with a swinging rope, climbing area, and great, sturdy slide that accommodates grownups as easily as five-year-olds. Little ones enjoy the small animals, too, and if they haven't been sidetracked by kittens, roosters, or lambs, may make it to the kitchen with a few eggs for the next day's breakfast. The entire staff joins in helping out with the kids, taking them panning for gold, giving them a hand cranking out some homemade ice cream, or teaching them the basics of horse care.

RIGHT, above. The ridin[skills of all guests a[checked out in the ring b[fore rides leave the ranc[Below, the children a[taken on an "overnigh[that includes a teepee a[marshmallows. The camp[across a meadow by the ed[of a pine fore[

mile dirt road—overlooks a wide expanse of lush, green grazing meadow. Monday's rides begin here, and as the week progresses, riders head farther and farther into Routt National Forest. The meadow-mountain blend and the small number of riders per wrangler—usually no more than four or five—create memorable opportunities to lope and explore some superb countryside.

The views from the eight spruce-log cabins overlook the grassland to the foothills beyond. Arranged in a well-spaced row and tucked into the first line of aspens at one end of the meadow, the accommodations resemble small houses. Some have fireplaces, some upstairs and downstairs bedrooms, and all have kitchen-

The Jacuzzi

WYOMING

PARADISE GUEST RANCH

BUFFALO, WYOMING

The powerful draw of the open range

ONCE you've loped through Paradise's high mountain meadows flecked with yellow arrowleaf balsam, white field chickweed, and blue lupine, you'll question the derivation of the word *paradise*, which at one time meant "an enclosed park." With a good horse beneath him and nothing but undulating hills unfolding ahead, even the most timid rider can sense the powerful draw of openness here.

A fifteen-minute ride from the ranch carries guests into remote territory where, the brochure states, "elk bugle and deer graze, where pine squirrels chatter at you from the treetops and an occasional moose stands belly deep in clear mountain lakes." And sure enough a cow moose appeared

to a solitary hiker on his first day at the ranch. Birders, too, will appreciate Paradise. "We get our share of hawks, a lot of redtail and sparrowhawks, golden eagles, occasionally a bald eagle," says Jim Anderson, manager of this 158-acre ranch in the shadow of the Bighorn Mountains.

Not long ago, the few ramshackle buildings that remained on the property were condemned. Breathing life into a dream, chairman of the board Raymond Plank arranged for Minneapolis-based Apache Oil to buy and refurbish the ranch. From 1982 through 1985, workmen renovated the existing structures, sandblasting both interiors and exteriors, adding modern water lines, providing new foundations, picture windows, and more. Over one

PRECEDING PAGE. Manager Jim Anderson's award-winning mule team pulling a chuck wagon out on the range to meet a ride for dinner. LEFT. Jim (right) joins wranglers around a campfire. ABOVE. Looking down on the ranch during an early morning breakfast ride.

million dollars were poured into the cabins; another million revamped the core facilities, the rec room, and the stunning two-story lodge that houses the French Creek Saloon, with its vintage Wurlitzer jukebox and trophy heads on the walls.

The décor in the eighteen one- to three-bedroom cabins more closely resembles that of an urbane country house than a rustic cow camp. Indian blankets bring out the best of Shaker chairs or a blonde-wood English butler's table. Impeccably appointed, the cabins, owned by individual investors, create a standard unparalleled at most other dude ranches. Amenities include individual heat con-

Rides travel across high mountain meadows, into pine forests, by cascading streams.

Managers Jim and Leah Anderson met while working at a dude ranch.

ning mules to the 80 head of horses; that feel equally at home in the dense forest or by a cascading stream as they do on the open mesa. Limited to about six people per group, the morning jaunts usually see family and friends riding together; afternoon excursions divide up by riding ability. The local wranglers enhance the rides, spinning yarns of bears and brawn. Jim and Leah encourage the staff to mix with the guests, and it's not unusual to hear intent conversations at the family-style meals.

Even the children join in, asking what it's like to be a real cowboy—or cowgirl. Dottie Knickerbocker, the children's wrangler, and Patty Tolman, the kids' counselor, keep the youngsters busy. A horseshoe tournament, sawdust sculpture, painting with dandelions, and a kid's overnight—these only begin the list that Patty, a former day-care center supervisor, draws from. When combined with the family activities—fishing, bonfires, talent show, square dance, picnic trail rides—visitors don't ever have to leave the ranch.

trol, fireplace, kitchenette, dining table, and living room.

Jim and Leah Anderson, congenial managers of Paradise, came here after running the Mud Creek Mule Parlor, their own hay- and sleigh-ride business. They've added their comely, prize-win-

ABOVE. The wrangler crew takes time out to pose for a group portrait. LEFT. The impeccable log cabins are stylishly furnished.

The chuck wagon cookout.

SPEAR-O-WIGWAM RANCH

SPEAR-O-WIGWAM RANCH

SHERIDAN, WYOMING

Guests are attracted by the intimate seclusion

EFT. The spectacular dge is designed like a and wigwam, and houses e living and dining rooms. ELOW. Ranch managers m and Barbara Niner, ho grew up here in the ig Horn.

THE approach to Spear-O-Wigwam rates among the best drives in the United States. The first five miles of rough gravel road wind through the northern end of the Ponderosa pine ecosystem, past trees standing like an army of soldiers at attention, through accordion folds of earth carpeted in velvet green. The excitement builds as the route climbs and the road disappears into open sky. As the road turns, aspens give way to more pines and spruce, until the land breaks and then you're among open bluebell-dotted meadows flanked by the snow-spotted Bighorns. At this point the road improves somewhat for the last only slightly less spectacular ten miles to the ranch.

Spear-O-Wigwam's intimate seclusion attacts guests who want the unadulterated pleasures of riding and being in the middle of the woods. "You don't have to do anything here. You don't have to get up if you don't want to. People who feel comfortable enough can even ride by themselves," says cowboy-manager Jim Niner, "if they know the trails and have proven themselves."

Originally a fishing camp and the retreat where in 1928 Ernest Hemingway completed *A Farewell to Arms*, Spear-O-Wigwam is set on seventeen acres in the middle of Bighorn National Forest. Just sixteen miles in, on the other side of the Cloud Peak Wilderness, lies the hidden, permanent pack-trip camp. Terry Punt, a teacher during school season, spends his summers in the timberland, welcoming weekly guests who opt for an overnight. Barbara Niner, who shares the ranch responsibilities with her husband, packs clean linens for the iron bedframes in the spacious tents on wooden platforms. Sometimes she'll include steaks or shrimp, which are second only to the wonderful food that the chef cooks up back at the ranch.

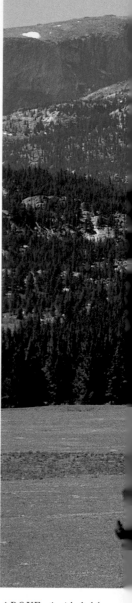

"We call the camp the Beaver Lake Country Club," says Jim. Not only is there a tent sauna and some of the best fishing lakes in the region, but Terry has packed in golf clubs and set up a three-hole golf course, a visible sign of the good humor and congeniality that boosts Spear-O-Wigwam into the ranks of a dude ranch par excellence.

Jim will keep surprising those who coax him. He's gained film credits, a reputation as a good local singer—and yodeler—and a twenty-five-plus year history as a cowhand. His studies in botany, range management, and animal husbandry left room for him to learn to rope, and if you're lucky he may teach you some of the basics. The wranglers, among them the Niners' son Curt, merit notice as well. Most of them hail from range country and are well-versed practitioners of cowboy arts.

ABOVE. A ride led by a wrangler and pack horse head out for the Big Horn National Forest which surrounds the ranch.

LEFT, above. A break during a ride gives everybody a rest. Below, Jim and his son (at left) with fellow wranglers.

Although the ranch chooses not to offer a structured schedule of activities, "once a week we have a picnic ride and usually an evening cookout," Barbara says. "Occasionally there'll be a breakfast cookout." "We've got a lake, too," adds Jim, "but you'll freeze your tail off if you swim in it. But the kids do it." Most families plan to spend a lot of quality time together, bring their own babysitter, or call in advance to arrange for child care.

Accommodations reflect the philosophy of the ranch: Simple and unpretentious, they're done up with the basics. Some have braided rugs; others, wall-to-wall carpeting. Vintage pine-log beds establish the decor scheme in several rooms; a wood stove occupies central focus in one living area; and a row of cabins stand within earshot of Giggling Creek. The octagonal, cathedral-ceilinged living room in the main house, however, steals people's hearts. It's hard to get guests to their beds once they've settled into the homey comfort of the couches scattered around the freestanding lava-rock fireplace that consumes five-foot-long logs.

CASTLE ROCK CENTRE

CODY, WYOMING

For those who love the outdoors

BESIDES offering a first-class horse program under the able supervision of ranch foreman Bill Snow, Castle Rock invites its guests to try kayaking, rock climbing, fishing, hiking with pack llamas, archery, and more. The Wieters family, who owns the ranch, has been involved with the camping industry for more than twenty-five years. Nelson received his master's degree in camping administration from George Williams University and has never left the field. A teacher and natural scientist, he set up one of the country's first outdoor education programs for high school students. The adult ranch reflects his years of experience with the children's camps.

Guests can sit back and watch the excitement as others stretch their physical limits, or they can participate to whatever degree they like. One teenager volunteered to climb the main house's chimney as demonstrated by the instructors. Petrified on the way up, she continued the lesson and descended with a tremendous grin on her face. The next day after her morning ride, she tried learning an Eskimo roll in the pool. Before the week was over, she navigated her way down the south fork of the Shoshone River by raft, hiked through Yellowstone National Park with well-informed guides, and learned how to lope.

"We consider our staff part of our guest experience," says Robin Sprague, Nel-

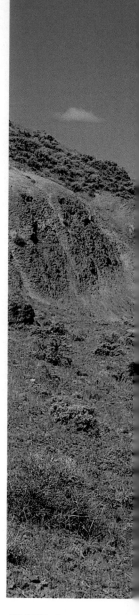

ABOVE. Riders traverse the sage desert over land that John Colter explored in the early 1800s. LEFT. The ranch's pack llamas, used for day hikes. Castle Rock is seen in the distance at far left.

Wranglers Lindsey Ringler and Bill Snow. At the nearby Cody rodeo, Lindsey often enters the calf roping events, while Bill's speciality is bull riding.

son's daughter and managing host of the lodges. The crew members are intelligent, alert, and patient. In addition, all are certified as Emergency Medical Technicians. Safety standards above what the government requires and an outstanding track record allows the ranch to offer its wide array of activities.

If all that doesn't suggest that Castle Rock delivers an unusual vacation, the landscape will. The family spent two and a half years looking for just the right site. They found it on the banks of the Shoshone River, which borders one mile of their property. Looking in the other direction, you gaze out over desert-to-alpine topography, sage-framed rock outcrops reminiscent of Monument Valley with snow-streaked mountains in the distance. Castle Rock itself rises up out of classic wild west country as if a child had built a sand castle on a mound of dry earth.

A good day's expenditure of energy deserves good food. Stir-fried vegetables

ABOVE. The cookout on Carter Mountain invariably ends with music. LEFT. Cabin arrangements vary from one room with twin beds to king-bedded suites with fireplaces.

RIGHT. Bill and Robin Wieters Sprague, the managing hosts for the dude ranch program at Castle Rock. *BELOW.* Our author, Naomi Black, is the lead paddler on a rafting expedition on the south fork of the Shoshone River, right on the ranch's property.

with baby shrimp has a place on the menu with the more traditional steak and potatoes. "We don't use any canned vegetables," says Robin. "Occasionally we'll have to use canned fruits or frozen vegetables," she adds, but you'll never notice. A fresh, enticing salad bar accompanies every lunch and dinner. This is one ranch that easily accommodates vegetarians.

The same care goes into the housing arrangements. The simple decor includes hand-painted curtains with traditional Indian design borders. A Pendleton blanket covers each bed. Prospective guests who request information receive a floor plan for each of the cabins, a nice touch that minimizes surprises.

Those who love the outdoors and the company of people who share that passion won't be disappointed here. If anything, they'll come away thrilled beyond all expectations.

GRIZZLY RANCH

CODY, WYOMING

The homestead of a former rodeo rider

ON THE other side of Cody, just off Route 14/20, with accommodations for fifteen guests, Grizzly Ranch specializes in providing a modest ranch vacation. "Because of our size, we don't have to be structured. We don't go on the river float every Thursday afternoon. We go when it's hot," says Rick Felts, a blustery character who loves to tell stories.

"Most of my education," Rick says, "came down the rodeo road," and it has served him well. In addition to being past president of the Cody Outfitters Association, he has helped design "a guest saddle with enough swell and cantle for security plus the comfort of a padded seat." Although Rick has given up bucking horses for dudes, he still seems the picture of a rodeo cowboy.

An overnight, included in the seven-day tariff, stands out as the week's high point. Rick's two wranglers help him load up the foam pads, sleeping bags, and tents along with all the dinner and break-fast fixings: beef stew, Kool-Aid, home-

made bread and chocolate cake, pancakes, eggs, sausage, coffee, and hot chocolate—even toothpicks in a tabasco sauce jar. Once the tents are up, most of the guests head out on another ride, perhaps up to Log Pile Ridge, where the logs were cut for Rick's house. The overlook affords an extraordinary view into the valley. Don't expect to lope here; the terrain is steep and rugged, perfect for sightseeing.

As the night sky envelops the mountains, Rick builds a bonfire that illuminates his circle of eager listeners. With the perfect voice for recitation, he plunges into the classics of cowboy poetry and regional stories. Young and old, families and singles join in toasting the occasion with a golden-browned or charred black marshmallow. The next morning, those who want to can help water and curry the horses.

When not camping under the stars, guests bundle up in snug little cabins that capture Rick's conviction that simplicity is best. Appointments include metal-frame beds, cinderblock-and-board bookcases, and maybe a trophy head on the wall or quilts on the beds.

Homespun meals follow the same tra-

The lodge at the ranch dates from the 1920s.

dition. Freshly baked English muffins or oatmeal cookies appear on the table as readily as fried chicken or brisket with horseradish sauce. Rick's longtime partner Kim Holmes oversees the cabins and cooking. When she's not busy she often stops to give out recipes or talk to the children. The ranch can arrange for babysitters if guests call in advance. On-site, the kids discover the swings, the likely spots to find petrified wood, and the stocked fish pond.

Rick and Kim encourage their guests to visit the Cody Nite Rodeo and the Buffalo Bill Historical Center (BBHC)—a superb collection of western art and artifacts—by planning it into the ranch schedule. Neither should be missed. The BBHC incorporates the Buffalo Bill Museum, Plains Indian Museum, Whitney Gallery of Western Art, and the Winchester Arms Museum. One day barely does it justice. You may have to stay on at Grizzly just to go back. Rick will also take visitors who opt for a five- or seven-day plan at the ranch, to Trail Town, a fascinating assembly of 25 buildings that date from 1879 to 1900. Among them are the outlaw cabin of Butch Cassidy and the Sundance Kid, a saloon with bullet holes in the door, and a one-room schoolhouse.

LEFT. The ranch rates include a rafting trip on the Shoshone River.
RIGHT. The Buffalo Bill Historical Center is nearby, and Rick recommends at least one visit.

ABSAROKA RANCH

DUBOIS, WYOMING

A picture perfect oasis surrounded by sage

AFTER eighteen years in the state Budd Betts considers himself a Wyomingite. He deserves to. Besides turning his ranch into a picture-perfect oasis in the middle of sun-drenched sage plains—and capturing the romance that goes with it—he's a self-taught weather buff and sits on the board of Wyoming's Outdoor Council. He and his wife Emi have settled into the land as if their families had been original homesteaders.

"I came out with my parents and loved it [the land]," Budd says. The memorable landscape here affords resplendent, unspoiled vistas in every direction, with rich, varied riding opportunities. Beyond the rolling hills to the south of the ranch,

the rugged peaks of the Wind River range loom on the horizon. To the north, running east-west, the spectacular Absarokas jut up. And there at the base, at the headwaters of the Wind River, stands the stylish and tranquil Absaroka Ranch.

Nestled by the edge of an aspen grove, three of the four cabins define corners of a rectangular green; the last bungalow rests just beyond the tidily-fenced quadrangle. Each cabin sports its own personality. Two pineapple-poster twins, a bunk bed, and two double beds share one cabin's spaciousness. A high ceiling and varnished pine walls distinguish Six-Point, while pine log beds and exposed cut pine walls characterize Five Mile. One smaller new cabin embraces the charm of a coun-

LEFT. Owners Budd and Emi Betts at their corral.

ABOVE. The Absaroka Mountains tower above the ranch, which, at 8,000 feet, is surrounded by the Disney Ranch and the Shoshone National Forest.

ABOVE. Two of the thirty-odd riding horses, which include Appaloosas, paints, bays, and a full sampling of western bred mounts. RIGHT. The wranglers.

Impromptu roping contest.

try bed-and-breakfast. All boast wall-to-wall carpeting, individual heating controls, and new quilted comforters.

Emi's gaiety and good nature, revealed in the accommodations, also leave their mark in the dining room. "I worked as a cook for many years," says Emi. From the menu presentation to the final, delicious result, the level of professionalism shines through. Each afternoon and evening, a green chalkboard foretells the goodies to come. One Saturday night dinner consisted of chilled cucumber cream soup, broccoli amandine, seafood *en croute*, fresh wheat rolls, wine, and a surprise dessert.

The caliber of the riding matches the wonderful food and comfy surroundings. The ranch has enough staff to be able to send guests out on individual rides. One group of three came back excited that they'd seen and heard a troubled coyote barking and a surprised antelope snorting. Wildlife watchers rejoice when they're here. The Wind River range hosts the world's largest herd of bighorn sheep. Mule deer, elk, moose, black bear, trumpeter swans, and golden eagles also inhabit those heights. And in the Absarokas you can see sandhill cranes and bald eagles if you're lucky.

Budd and Emi tailor the activities to guests' needs, so if you'd rather cast for fish, you just have to let them know. The favorite excursion of visitors may be the all-day ride to Trail Lake where a cliff drops off 1,500 feet. The nights come alive Monday with a square dance, Tuesday with a rodeo in Riverton, and Wednesday with a steak ride into the forest. Expect a lively discussion with a modern-day buckskin-clad mountain man on Thursday. Then, if you still have energy left on Friday, you can seek out Dubois' nightlife. Saturday? Sit back and absorb the good times you've had here.

BITTERROOT RANCH

DUBOIS, WYOMING

"We ride harder than most ranches"

WE TEND to get a much more horse-oriented clientele here," says Mel Fox. "We ride harder than most ranches." In fact, with approximately one hundred horses for twenty-two guests, Bitterroot is the only ranch that customarily gives each guest two horses for the week; one for morning rides, the second for the afternoon. Bitterroot further distinguishes itself from more ordinary dude ranches with its Polish-cross breeding program. The Polish strain in their stallions adds sturdiness and docility to the Foxes' Arabians. Of the six horses born each year, Mel usually breaks four of them herself, two in the spring and two in the fall. "A hired hand breaks the other two and schools the ones that I break," says Mel.

Most guests ride with a western saddle and take part in the twice-weekly lessons. Advanced equestrians may prefer one of the half-dozen English saddles and will be sure not to miss Cynthia "Cinch" Schell's hard-hitting instruction. Lessons are often videotaped, which provides guests even more of a chance to better their skills.

The Foxes provide powerful incentive for improvement. Through their company called Equitour they offer riding

LEFT. The spectacular range for riding includes the Shoshone National Forest and borders the Wind River Indian Reservation. BELOW. Owners Mel and Bayard Fox with one of their two Arabian stallions. The other is shown to the right.

A typical ranch cabin.

vacations all over the world—from the rural countryside of Burgundian France to the desert of Egypt to the highlands of Kenya. This last trip they lead themselves. Mel grew up on a farm in Tanzania, speaks fluent Swahili, and is intimately acquainted with the game parks. Bayard Fox's background as a former CIA man obliged him to travel, so as a pair they are well-suited to opening the world to horse lovers and have made a great effort to include trips that highlight the horses in addition to the scenery. Portugal's ride, for example, employs powerfully built, regionally touted Lusitano horses.

The international influence can be felt strongly back at the ranch. Many French, Italian, and German guests discover the pull of the Wild West at Bitterroot, and they return year after year, recommending it to their friends, who in turn fall in love with the raw landscape and its mesmerizing attraction.

Even children are not immune, especially when they are taken up by Richard, the Foxes' seven-year-old who unlocks for them the doors of local wonder. It's not unusual to see Richard at the lead with several kids in tow heading for the stocked fish pond with a small inflatable boat and some simple fishing rods. The children can also hunt for arrowheads, prairie agate, petrified wood, and geodes or spend the morning learning how to groom, clean, and unsaddle their ponies.

Picnic rides go farther up into the mountains and sometimes cross over the timberline. If you opt to remain at the ranch for lunch, you can expect good, hearty food. The cabins, too, stand as solid models of comfort. Well spaced, some are hidden from view of the others. All have wood-burning stoves and/or electric heat.

An unusual addition to the dude ranch roster, Bitterroot is nonetheless steeped in the heritage of the West. On a clear day in early summer, you may even get to help hold down the calves for branding!

LEFT. Mel doing the rounds on the ranch's jumping course.

ABOVE. *No, you're not seeing things. This is a photograph of a horseback trip through Mel's native East Africa. Through Equitour, the Foxes offer horseback trips through France, Portugal, Kenya, and other countries.*

The Foxes' son, Richard.

LAZY L & B RANCH

DUBOIS, WYOMING

An extraordinarily lovely setting

THE road approaching Lazy L & B winds down into the cottonwood-studded bottomlands of the Wind River's East Fork. In the waning sunlight, this valley reflects the colors of its striking red rock walls, walls that become even more alluring up close when their intricate structure becomes visible. The lush green and the stark red create a contrast unmatched in the surrounding area.

Once known as "Scotch Valley" because its first settlers in the nineteenth century were sheepherders from Scotland, this region offers a widely varied terrain. Riders can follow the meandering river by the sandstone hills, lope across high plains by an old homestead cabin, or trot across alkaline flats into cool, green forests. The valley is nestled in by the Wind River Indian Reservation on the east and the State Elk Feeding Refuge and the Shoshone National Forest on the west. Bordering the elk refuge is the Didiers' Upper Ranch, whose headquarters is a homestead cabin that serves as a picnic place where guests spread out with baloney salad sandwiches and fruit, and where some of the youngsters hold trading sessions offering one chocolate

ABOVE. The ranch site, the only place in the valley where the red sandstone is exposed. LEFT. Trail rides traverse an 11,000 acre elk feeding refuge and private cattle land.

Owner Bernard Didier, who bought the ranch 20 years ago.

Daughter Leota and husband tether their horses in an aspen grove.

creme cookie for two vanilla stuffed treats.

The horses and tack remain at the Upper Ranch every Wednesday and Thursday—to vary the next day's rides and to furnish a kickoff for more hardy riders—while most guests pile into the trucks and travel back and forth in the ranch's four-wheeled vehicles. If they want, children—and adults—may stay overnight at the Upper Ranch or in the adjoining forest in tents and sleeping bags. Kids also enjoy the hayrides and the chuckwagon dinner by the heated pool. Most nights children eat early with the crew, who keep them busy while the grownups enjoy the happy hour hospi-

tality of the Didiers' ranch home. Don't be surprised to see your wrangler cleaned up and asking you whether you'd like iced tea, lemonade, or coffee. The guys do double-duty here, as do the cabin girls who help with kitchen chores.

Authentic log cabins, many of them historic, range in size and style from the stunning split-level Mountain View to single, double, and triple cabins with porches from which guests look out over surrounding pastures to mountain ranges beyond. White walls with wood slats lend a British half-timbered look to the otherwise simple ranch house affectionately called the Ponderosa. The building serves as the dining hall and general gathering place for guests.

Run by outspoken owners Bernard and Leota, Lazy L & B can burst into frenetic activity before a scheduled event. Schedules and riding are flexible and adapted to the individual preferences and abilities of guests. All in all, the Didiers offer a lively getaway in an extraordinarily lovely setting.

ABOVE. Loping over the undulating hills, with an incredible western vista in the background. LEFT. Wranglers at the corral. RIGHT. A modern substitute for cooling off at the old swimmin' hole.

TRAIL CREEK RANCH

WILSON, WYOMING

An oasis of authentic western life

RANCH owner Elizabeth Woolsey embraces life with remarkable gusto. Like Amelia Earhart and Althea Gibson in their days, Woolsey captured the excitement and vigor of the sporting community before World War II. Her reputation as one of the first women technical mountain climbers is exceeded only by her standing as a member in the National Ski Hall of Fame. Competing for the 1936 Olympic ski team and winning the open downhill in the 1939 National Championships begin Betty's list of extraordinary accomplishments. Today, she funnels her energy into managing her ranch. She especially enjoys irrigating her hayfields, which produce plenty of high quality hay to feed her seventy-odd stock when the ranch is buried in snow. Often, guests' first glimpse of Betty is her petite figure clad in workclothes and high rubber boots.

Born in Albuquerque but raised primairly in Connencticut, Betty writes in her book *Off the Beaten Track*, "From childhood, my delight in simply being alive was intensified with every foot I put between myself and sea level." At 6,280 feet, Trail Creek Ranch nestles into a quiet niche at the foot of Teton Pass. The Snake River Range lies to the south; to the east is the high meadow country of the Gros Ventres. To the north, the Tetons jut dramatically up from the valley floor named Jackson Hole. When Betty first saw the peaks, she writes, "It was a scene to make the heart beat faster."

Guests at Trail Creek may ride into

LEFT. One of the joys of Trail Creek is riding through meadows of wild flowers. RIGHT. The 1920s era barn, which holds 40 tons of hay as well as tack for the horses and pack trips.

the mountains and meadows along paths whose names are as evocative as the places themselves: Cascade Canyon, Lake Solitude, Skyline and Paintbrush trails. Day rides nearer the ranch satisfy less adventurous riders.

Betty stresses that "a ranch is a ranch is a ranch" and not a resort. Riding is the primary scheduled event, although guests may arrange to fish, hike, or borrow a canoe to explore the lakes in nearby Grand Teton National Park. Expect to amuse yourselves in the evening by sharing an early nightcap with other guests in the lodge living room or in the cardroom bar, where Betty's scrapbooks fill more than one bookshelf. An impressive library and a bumper pool table upstairs each attract a following.

Guests turn in to attractive, cozy cabins designed to withstand winter chill. Decor differs in each, from pale-blue stenciled twin beds and enclosed summer porch in one to another family cabin with an upstairs sleeping area.

ABOVE. Riding is the prime activity at Trail Creek. LEFT. Most of the cozy log cabins are winterized to withstand the long Wyoming winters.

ABOVE. The six experienced wranglers in charge of riding and pack trips.

BELOW. A ranch expert teaches a guest the rudiments of fly fishing.

Trail Creek "started as a house party of friends . . . an informal arrangement," says Betty, who came for the skiing and ended up with a lifetime commitment to ranching in the magnificent Teton country. The majority of Trail Creek's guests come from word-of-mouth recommendations by friends and former guests.

Along with a crew of twelve, including six wranglers, Betty, Muggs Schultz, and Marian "Sis" McKean Wigglesworth form a powerful triumvirate that attends to the details of running the ranch. Muggs, a Jackson native, almost made the 1948 Olympic ski team. Sis met Betty in the 1930s when they skiied together in Europe; she now tends a magnificent garden, watering and weeding the seven kinds of lettuce and other vegetables that appear in season on the dinner table. The three truly personify Trail Creek Ranch, an oasis of authentic western life outside of the tourist attractions and ski lodges that characterize present-day Jackson Hole.

HEART SIX RANCH

MORAN, WYOMING

The infectious vitality of the Garnick family

THE vitality of Heart Six is infectious, and it stems directly from the Garnick family, who thrive on activity. Bill, a longtime cattleman and auctioneer, knew Harry Knight and Roy Rogers. His wife Billie enlisted the help of these friends and, after many years as an announcer at Indian rodeos, became the first woman Rodeo Cowboys of America rodeo announcer. The travel required by the job didn't slow Billie down. She received her masters degree in business administra- tion, then worked for the Shoshone, Arapaho, and Navajo tribes before she took off for Europe to help develop tourism and economic development in five western states.

The Garnick's son Cameron inherited his mother's dynamism. As Billie says, "Our boys learned horsemanship from Bill and showmanship from me." Cameron juggles his time between running the ranch and furthering his acting career. He has appeared in a mini-series with Richard Chamberlain, *Rocky IV*, and the

ABOVE. The horses are herded from the corrals to pasture twice daily. LEFT Children's programs keep the kids busy and smiling. These two are holding baby Sanen goats. RIGHT. Two steps down from the dining room, the living room show cases a variety of trophy heads.

television series *Vegas*. With his wife Vicki, he bought the old Jackson Hole Theater in Jackson and treats the ranch guests to such extravaganzas as *The Sound of Music*. The building itself, the second oldest in town, is a delight; with its pressed tin ceilings, red-velvet-draped piano, and crystal chandeliers, it recalls a time when saloon doors swung open for mustachioed gunfighters and the mail arrived by Pony Express or stagecoach.

By theater night—Tuesday—the children at the ranch play as if they'd sealed their newfound friendship as blood brothers. Kids think the G-rated program is great. From old John Wayne movies to

caller-led outdoor square dancing to hayrides and a teepee overnight, they participate without coaxing. There are always a few who take time out of the breakfast ride to brave the cold waters of the Buffalo River and thus become members of the Polar Bear Club. For the more sedate, Heart Six offers easy nature walks, an evening with a Shoshone Bannock family or a member of the Mountain Man Society, and campfire sing-alongs.

The ranch's location, just a few miles from the entrance to Grand Teton National Park, adds even more options to the activity menu. Canoe rentals, Snake River raft trips, and guided fishing floats take advantage of the scenic wonders, while the commercial establishments offer an aerial tram, Alpine slide, and varied shopping. The Pack Saddle gallery, a colorful Indian gift shop right next door to the ranch, extends a thirty percent discount on silver jewelry to ranch guests.

With so much to do, Heart Six guests still make time for more traditional pursuits. Everyone goes to the rodeo, and very few people miss out on a day of riding. After the wrangler, a Wyoming native, pointed out a camouflaged sage hen and stopped to listen to the melancholy call of a sandhill crane, one guest noted that "every ride is a nature ride."

ABOVE. These wranglers are professional rodeo riders as well, and look the part.

ABOVE. Cameron and Vicki Garnick run the musical theater in Jackson, and a show is included as part of the ranch activities.

BELOW. A wagon pulled by a team of black percherons takes nonriders to the breakfast site on the banks of the Buffalo River.

MONTANA

ABOVE. In this great old ranch house the family furniture dates back to the 1800s. The style of the cabins, right, could be called "western rustic."

PRECEDING PAGE. With the Crazy Mountains in the background, wranglers and guests of the Lazy K move cattle to fresher pasture.

LEFT. A light in the window once symbolized an open door, the cornerstone of western hospitality.

LAZY K BAR RANCH

BIG TIMBER, MONTANA

One of the oldest and most beautiful dude ranches in the country

LAZY K BAR holds the distinction of being one of the first dude ranches in the U.S. and the oldest in Montana—not to mention being one of the most beautiful anywhere. Since 1922 the Van Cleve family has welcomed guests to what is now their 26,000-acre spread. Barbara, the matriarch of the family, and three of her children, Tack, Barbie, and Carol, run the ranch as a family affair. Tradition becomes tangible at this granddaddy of working guest ranches.

Tack's father Spike—the late Paul Van Cleve III, a Harvard-educated man who lived close to the land—became famous for his anecdotes of dude ranching. One of his stories won him a Western Heritage Award from the National Cowboy Hall of Fame. When at the ranch ask to see

the film *Spike: A Montana Horseman*. The documentary seems more like a home movie; and in the company of his family, Spike's presence can be felt as if he had sneaked into the room when the lights were turned down. Barbara, too, radiates warmth and a certain robust élan that belies her age. The undisputed doyenne of the ranch, she speaks with clarity and humor about the days past, including when, as newlyweds, she and Spike had to make their remaining thirteen dollars last from September to June.

In his own inimitable way, Tack has inherited the family talent for story-telling. He delights in the history of his family and of the land they settled on. Barbie's no slouch either, although to hear her stories you have to catch her first. Even better than her stories, however, are her handsome, professional photographs, which adorn the walls of some cabins and are exhibited on notecards at the store.

Carol spends so much time behind the scenes that you may not see her at first; she's responsible for the ranch-fresh beef, vegetables, and eggs that grace Lazy K Bar meals and for the wildflowers and turn-down service in the cabins.

Guest accommodations range from charming one-room cabins without bath to wonderfully rustic four-bedroom lodges, all with at least one bath. Every cabin holds a treasure of some sort: a primitive

painting, a rug woven with yarn taken from Civil War uniforms, a 1941 Zenith radio. The appointments, too, add a real coziness that makes these cabins seem more like homes; more often than not you'll encounter willow, wicker, or pole furniture and a fireplace or Franklin stove.

The main house reflects the character of the family just as the cabins do. Upon entering you'll probably notice the 1883 Brunswick pool table with stunning inlay and leather pockets that was saved from a fire in the 1920s. The Pony Express bag in the store, an original, still transports mail to town—via truck. The details—and the stories—are legion.

But it's riding that's all-important at the Lazy K Bar. "We've been breeding and raising our own horses here since 1880," says Tack. Many of the one hundred-head herd have thoroughbred blood in them, and as Barbie is quick to note, "Most of the horses are registered." It all makes for spirited and extraordinary riding. You can lope through wildflower meadows, move cattle to a different pasture, explore Alpine lakes, climb the ridges, and rest by waterfalls. All-day excursions go out as the guests see fit. As for an overnight ride, "We'll do it for just two guests or twenty," says Barbie.

Although no planned activities appear on a schedule, guests can expect a square dance, a Sunday morning breakfast walk, and a moonlight ride to Barbie's place for a cookout. Kids from six to fourteen ride with a children's wrangler and customarily eat at a separate table. For tots five and under, the Van Cleves suggest bringing a nurse or nanny.

FT, above. Horses ssing a stream from the ral area to the overnight ture. Below, Barbie Van ve stands in the middle our wranglers, who are hly experienced, perform- all the duties on a king ranch.

RIGHT. The Van Cleve clan (from left to right): Barbie, matriarch Barbara, Carol, and Tack, a former president of the Dude Ranchers Association.

63
RANCH

LIVINGSTON, MONTANA

Guests can lope through high meadows with ease

THE 63 Ranch, a stalwart pioneer of working dude ranches, became a National Historic Site in the early 1980s. Nestled at the foot of the north slope of the Absaroka Mountains, just one mile from the Absoraka-Beartooth Wilderness, it carries on a legacy that began in 1929 as a vision of three young Minnesotans: Paul Christensen, his brother Elmer, and his sister Jo.

Today the ranch runs under the capable direction of Paul's wife Jinnie and daughter and son-in-law, Sandra and Bud Cahill. When Jinnie first met Paul, she was a guest at a neighboring dude ranch, the Triangle 7. After a few years of courting, Paul inspired his eastern sweetheart to come west again, this time to be his bride. The River View cabin where Jinnie stayed still welcomes visitors, only now it is part of the 63 Ranch.

The setting can certainly awaken romance. Visitors to the ranch enjoy the quiet, rustic setting at the head of Mission Creek Canyon. "It's so beautiful here. I want to draw it all inside me and take it home," said one guest as she looked out over the

ABOVE. The road to 63 Ranch provides one of the most inviting approaches to any ranch in the west. LEFT. Guests wait outside the corral for wranglers to check their cinches.

Three generations of ranchers: Virginia Christensen with daughter Sandra Cahill, son-in-law Bud Cahill, and grandson Jeff.

LEFT. An old ranch building preserved for posterity, along with a grindstone for sharpening axes.

LEFT. An invitingly warm and rustic ranchhouse interior of the kind you dream about. BELOW. The ranch house from the outside.

countryside, the Crazy Mountains rising in the distance.

Although guests can lope through the high meadows with ease, past cows and tumbledown homestead shacks, many choose the all-day ride to Shell Mountain as their favorite; the "mountain" is really a nine-mile ridge of nine peaks where on a rest stop children can typically find fossils.

Sandra and the wranglers each lead rides every day but Sunday, the horses' day off. "We often don't decide what's up until that day." Guests can and do help with currying and unsaddling the horses. And when there's a ranch chore to do, many like to help out, whether it's checking on a new foal or moving the small herd of Hereford/Angus cross cows.

A low-keyed atmosphere prevails, reflecting Bud and Sandra's softspoken ways, which quietly capture the loyalties of adults and children alike. Kids often join in with the grown-ups, playing pool, jumping in the swimming hole, and trying to sit still during the wagon ride. When there's no square dancing, after-dinner activity tends to the quiet side, with guests reading or playing bridge in front of the fireplace. Or signing their names on the moose hides that, like white casts, serve as great graffiti backgrounds.

When it's time to retire, head off to a cabin that may house a piece of uncle Don Hindman's western fir- and pine-knot Molesworth furniture with designs of moose, birds in flight, or cowboys. Simple yet comfortable and clean, the rooms boast soft woolen blankets, feather pillows, a complimentary bandanna for each guest, information on how to ride a horse correctly, and a slender inspirational volume on wildflowers that Sandra wrote in memory of her father.

The Molesworth furniture showcased in the dining room—and the brightly colored, original Fiestaware—prompted one frequent return guest to remark, "Everything's still the same." The quality of the food remains consistently good, too, with traditional ranch standbys such as Dutch meatloaf and apple crisp sharing table space with Sandra's updated recipes for curry dip and fruit-and-cottage-cheese-based salad.

NINE QUARTER CIRCLE RANCH

GALLATIN GATEWAY, MONTANA

Maintaining Kelsey family traditions

IF YOU'RE looking for a family vacation where children will come away with lasting friendships and where adults can get away and ride on their own, this is the ranch. The children's program offers something for everyone. Babysitters take care of the under-six crowd, supervising the playground antics, leading the bigger tots on a gentle horse, or organizing a pageant. The six- to nine-year-olds flock around the kiddie wrangler to learn the basics of horse sense and riding. Even the ten-and-up set have their own group activities. Kids of all ages delight in trying to pet one of the 200-odd rabbits or a colt that's relaxing in front of the cabins.

Owners Kim and Kelly Kelsey follows many of the traditions that his father set when the elder Kelsey presided over the ranch. Children nine and under generally don't ride with their parents until Friday, an age-old formula that spurs the kids on to excel. Mealtimes as well are organized with the children seated separately, a custom that naturally encourages children to find new companions.

The Kelsey family's tenure at the ranch dates from 1946, when Kim's father fulfilled a dream by buying the Nine Quarter Circle; in the 1950s, he began breeding Appaloosas, first developed by the Nez Percé Indians for mountain riding. The enterprise continues to distinguish the

'T. Owners Kelly and Kelsey with one of two St. Bernards.

RIGHT. The trophy room boasts a huge stone fireplace that fills up one third of a wall. An elk head, bobcat skin, eagle, bighorn sheep head, and other trophies keep company with the coyote in the foreground.

*FT, above. Only capable
s attempt the ranch's
t difficult ride, the
lsey Killer." Below, the
a, orderly tack room, the
of a well-managed
h.*

ranch, and Nine Quarter Circle's 125 horses have earned a long-standing reputation for fineness, although they are not show horses. "The Appaloosas are awfully good at negotiating the trails," says Kim.

Riding begins on Monday morning. After an introductory lesson, groups of about ten or twelve go out by skill. As further instruction is needed, guests learn on the trail. Adults and kids over twelve sharpen their horse sense on the overnight. Kim warns, however, that "if you sign up for the all-day ride, be ready to

Corn bread, cakes, and other baked goods are made fresh daily.

Mares and foals are let out to pasture around the cabins in the afternoon.

The wrangler staff, which includes a children's counselor.

ride." Advanced equestrians look forward to the Kelsey Killer, an all-day outing that crosses rough terrain and may involve bushwacking.

Gentle slopes and open vistas characterize the landscape that the majority of the riders pass through, so loping is allowed. The ranch sits on land surrounded by the Gallatin National Forest, so you'll see plenty of wooded scenery. And deer. And hawks. And maybe even a moose or a few sandhill cranes.

Located on the Taylor Fork of the Gallatin River, Nine Quarter Circle lies at the center of "The Magic Hub," a ring of the best fly-fishing waters in the United States. Some of the fishing is accessible only by foot or horseback. Kim, who once worked as a rafting guide, can also set up a whitewater trip; "It's only a phone call away."

Nine Quarter Circle keeps its guests hopping. Each night at dinner the seat assignments change, so you'll meet everyone before the Saturday gymkhana and square dance. Most likely, however, you'll already have introduced yourself at the daily happy hour, at the Monday night softball game, or at one of the three outdoor meals. If not, one of the honor roll guests may introduce you. How do you get on the honor roll? Just keep coming back!

LONE MOUNTAIN RANCH

BIG SKY, MONTANA

An up-to-date,
ever-evolving western retreat

IN 1988 Barb Batey will begin her ninth year at Lone Mountain Ranch, a luxurious, holistic retreat run with such precision that, of 33 people on staff last year, only three were new. Typical of many crew members here, Barb considers the ranch her home. Her unfailing curiosity and enviable healthiness are also characteristic of Lone Mountain employees. Like the guests, the staff doesn't want to leave. They're having too much fun.

Another long-timer, Neil Navratil left a remunerative job in Minnesota to set up house at Big Sky. Although he functions as head chef, it's not unusual to see Neil on his mountain bike, pedaling his way to the foothills of the Spanish Peaks. Perhaps the fresh air stimulates his creativity; Neil produces some of the best food this side of the Hudson. Brie *en croute,* consommé Celestine, and a strawberries jubilee that flames down a spiralled and clove-studded orange peel stand forth as prime examples of the ambrosia whipped up in the Lone Mountain kitchen.

One of the newer wranglers came from a job on an intensive three-month wagon-

LEFT. Amy, the riding instructor, explains to a guest the cardinal rule for staying in the saddle: "Keep your heels down." RIGHT. The cabins are known for their spaciousness and comfort.

LEFT. Lone Mountain food is exceptional. Here chef Neil Navratil pours four liquers down a curlicue of clove-studded orange peel, flaming each on the way down.

RIGHT, above. Riding range in grand country. . . wranglers, below, are de . . . cated to the ranch and . . . activit . . .

train rehabilitation program that taught juvenile delinquents self-esteem and the rewards of hard work. Not only did he need to live, eat, and sleep horsemanship, but he had to demonstrate the human touch that reached out to those boys. The horse program here isn't comparably intense, of course, but the basics are the same. A relatively tame but beautifully sited cookout, and a breakfast ride, and a rodeo give the guests a more traditional taste of dude ranching. And a terrific children's program keeps the kids occupied.

And who is the pacesetter responsible for all this? Bob Schaap. A man with integrity, humor, and a touch that turns failing businesses to overnight successes. "I think we're really different," says Bob. "I love change. We encourage our crew to come up with new ideas. The guests never quite know what they're going to come back to." He oversees Lone Mountain with compassion and common sense, fostering in his workers a sense of independence that allows them to build their lives around the ranch.

Bob's commitment to quality—including the quality of the environment— extends to his guests and the ranch program and beyond. Barb, who received a masters degree in biochemistry and has

taken part in many of Yellowstone's interpretive workshops, leads the bird walks, trips to Yellowstone's backcountry, and most of the nature hikes. She also organizes an orienteering treasure hunt inspired by her work with the U.S. map-and-compass champion. Orvis endorses the ranch's fly fishing program, and the wranglers are quick to point out insensitive forestry policies that leave the land defiled.

In winter, Barb and other staff members turn into Nordic skiing guides, leading guests across country to witness Yellowstone's winter beauty.

A stay at Lone Mountain needn't change a guest's perspective on life. Some may not care to see beyond the hot tub and masseuse on call—but that's okay, too!

LEFT. At Lone Mountain, young riders grow fond of their horses.

DIAMOND J RANCH

ENNIS, MONTANA

The famous Big Sky country

AS YOU approach the Diamond J you'll understand why Montana is called "Big Sky Country." The twelve-mile dirt road passes through a flat stretch of grassland that shimmers in the light of a late summer evening. Not far away from the neighbor's range cows you may see a loping coyote chasing field mice or a hawk circling overhead. Situated at an elevation of 5,800 feet, nestled in the Madison range of mountains and enveloped by the Beaverhead National Forest, the trim, well-manicured Diamond J quietly continues a tradition that dates from 1931.

When owners Pete and Jinny Combs acquired the ranch in 1959, the region already held a special attraction for them; Jinny's father used to come here to hunt in the 1930s, and since Jinny and Peter were hometown sweethearts from Upland, California, both of them sometimes accompanied her father on the trips. They've explored China, golfed in Scotland, and gone on safari in Africa, but it's always to Ennis that they return.

Guests who visit them here feel almost part of a family reunion. Many older guests have been coming for ten or even twenty-plus years, and conversations at happy hour often renew old friendships with the appropriate introductions of children and grandchildren. As with most ranches, guests bring their own pre-dinner cocktails but once a week the Combs invite everyone up to their dramatically situated modern woodframe home. Whether you're partaking of Scotch and soda or soda water, don't miss the event.

ABOVE. A fine array of horses being driven to pasture. LEFT. A ride proceeding at a quiet walk through a lush pasture.

*The famous White Yellow-
stone Park touring bus.*

The stately sitting room of the main lodge.

Owners Jinny and Pete Combes.

The five-minute excursion to the house is unique. Felipe Acosta, who manages the ranch, chauffeurs the guests up to the Combs' in a 1937 White Yellowstone touring bus.

Felipe oversees the corrals, too, hiring some Mexican cowboys as well as the more traditional American wranglers. Riders can lope to their heart's content through the meadows by Jack Creek if they let Felipe know that's what they want to do. Jordan Ridge, another favorite ride, affords views of five mountain ranges, a panorama guests never tire of. Lessons, available on request, can be structured to individual needs.

Children of all ages happily find their niche here. "If anybody's from four on up, they ride," says Jinny. With a kids' wrangler and a staff of just over a dozen, trail rides are flexible; all-day treks can be arranged any or every day. "We have barbecue cookouts once a week, and frequent breakfast rides throughout the summer." Kids also like to go through Jinny's costume chest. When they do, anything can happen.

Nonriders can swim or enjoy indoor volleyball, indoor tennis, or skeet and trap shooting under the supervision of Olympic-trained instructor John Grochowski. Fishermen will want to take advantage of the permanent camp set up on the Madison River. With advance arrangements, guests can float, fish, stay the night, and fish again the next day.

Jinny and Peter Combs are marvelous hosts. At dinner Jinny guides guests to their seats, sometimes asking couples to sit apart "since you see each other all the time." With only occasional interruptions, as she rings a small bell to call one of the waitresses, conversation becomes lively, and everyone makes new friends before the night's over. The children, too, form quick alliances here, in part because they all eat together in a separate dining room at an earlier hour.

RIGHT, above. Guests of all ages take to riding like a duck to water. All the cabins, below, are similar in layout, with porches that make for easy socializing. BELOW. The ranch hands.

BEARTOOTH RANCH

NYE, MONTANA

A ranch that inspires loyalty among guests and crew

OUTSIDE the small town of Nye, on a dirt road that passes an unobtrusive working mine and winds deep into forested backcountry, you'll find Beartooth Ranch on a captivating plot of land that once belonged to the Crow Indians. Woodbine Falls drops into the mountains above the ranch, feeding into the fast-flowing Stillwater River, a challenging trout stream.

When prospectors first built Nye, it had one street with six frame-and-canvas saloons. "Schools were unnecessary, church unknown, and officers of the law unwanted," wrote one local historian.

Although the town has since settled down, the area retains its rough-and-tumble ambience.

Nye, noted for its diversity of ore—copper/nickel, chrome, and platinum/palladium—attracted more than the usual assembly of miners. Ellen Mouat, while visiting her uncle who owned many of the mining claims, "fell in love with the ranch and never got it out of my mind." Shortly after she married Jim Langston she discovered the ranch was for sale. With her two brothers, Ellen and Jim bought the ranch, and the couple moved onto the ranch as managers, first for the

ABOVE. The ranch has plenty of water, and the horses love it. LEFT. Wranglers in rain gear.

Jenny the mule being treated to an apple by an aspiring cowpoke.

family and now for the Stillwater Mining Company.

The Langstons instill a fierce loyalty in many of their crew—and their guests. "It may sound kind of corny, like a Louis L'Amour novel, but I ride for the brand," says Robin Hertzler, who first arrived as a guest when she was four years old. Her family returned for the next 14 years. Then Robin signed on to work with the Langstons and, after sweating it out as a cabin girl, cook, and assistant wrangler, became head wrangler. About three-quarters of the horses have been raised and bred on the ranch. "Because of the

ABOVE. The scenic but testing ride along the canyon.

LEFT, above. The fine old stone ranch house. Stone fireplaces in the cabins, below, provide warmth on mountain evenings.

way they're trained and treated, these horses make my job a lot easier," says Robin, who credits Ellen for the horses' good tempers.

Guests start out with a basic lesson, but can request more thorough instruction from Robin. "The best way to get fast riding in," says Ellen, "is to help the wranglers bring the horses in or take them out in the evening." Those who prefer can lope through the meadows, although most of the riding proceeds at a walk. And with good reason. The views of awesome rocky gorges and impressive canyon walls slow riders down.

Even the buildings blend in with the natural surroundings, especially Rendezvous, the fieldstone-and-log recreation hall, which has a feeling more commonly encountered in Adirondack lodges than western cabins. The nighttime entertainment usually centers around the fireside

pool and ping-pong tables in the high-raftered, capacious building. The ranch's recreation director takes care that children never get bored. Other activities include crafts, cookouts, lawn games, square dancing, a kids' melodrama, and an inspired treasure hunt on horseback. Two or three guests team up with a crew member, and the four or five teams head off to find and decipher clues. Limited to a trot, the different groups go in separate directions following clues that take them to a half dozen locations.

Usually the clues are hidden away from the accommodations, which range from motel-style units in a two-story wood-frame building to charming two-or-more-room log-and-stone cabins with fireplace or woodstove. A desk, an uncommonly comfortable easy chair, or a decorative detail add a cozy touch that makes the cabins seem that much more like home.

ABOVE. Owner Sarah Hollatz and Rick Stevenson high atop a hill overlooking the magnificent Circle Bar spread. LEFT. Guests ride through a carpet of blooming clover.

RIGHT. The luxurious ing room of the ranch hou

CIRCLE BAR GUEST RANCH

CIRCLE BAR GUEST RANCH

UTICA, MONTANA

The Old West and the new

SARAH HOLLATZ is admittedly outrageous at times, but to have come west and built what is probably the best *modern* dude ranch, she had to be a bit unconventional. Although the ranch has been around for over ninety years, Sarah bought it in 1982 and erected a main house that, while fitting into the landscape perfectly, could easily grace the pages of *Architectural Digest*. The ambience exudes energy; it practically crackles in the air. Sarah is a woman not of the old west but of the new.

Rick Stevenson, a fun-loving cowboy born and raised in the Utica-Hobson area, holds down the position of ranch manager. "He knows this country better than anyone else," boasts Sarah. Indeed, he and his brothers own more than 1,000 registered cows, and his family lays claim to popularizing the Angus breed in the state of Montana. Together, Rick and Sarah are quite a team.

Sarah has had her cattle for only a few years, but her first horse dates back to when she was two years old, which probably accounts for her unfailingly good eye for matching guests with mounts. She considers her best asset her ability to pick good horses and get rid of the bad ones. She weeds them out by personality. The "bad ones" sometimes become show horses because they're not really bad, they're just feisty.

With a modest breeding program, Sarah usually sees two or three new foals a year. The dude string now consists of about half registered quarterhorses, a few appaloosas, a few paints, and the rest grade horses.

Riding capitalizes on the open, expansive countryside that enchants visitors with its long views down the meadow. Only low foothills breaking the horizon line hint at the Little Belt Mountains, the range that's known as Charlie Russell country and the hiding place of a healthy herd of about 1,500 elk currently managed by the state.

The food from the Circle Bar kitchen is exceptional. Dick, the chef, worked as head of the Yellowstone food services for several years before opening his own restaurants. Here he's found a place for himself, contentedly cooking up such de-

ABOVE. The ranch buildings bask in the golden glow of the morning sunrise. RIGHT. The Circle Bar symbol over the barn door, where ranch hands Merrill and Sunny pose with Sarah and Rick.

Huevos Rancheros is part of Sunday brunch.

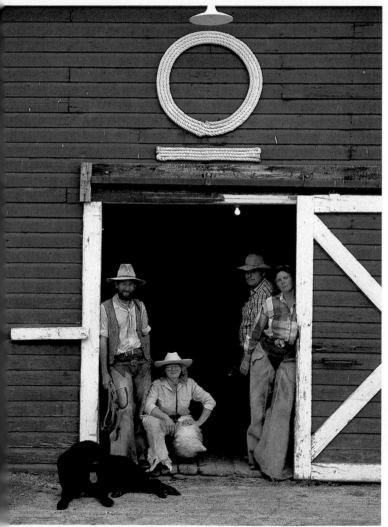

licacies as poppyseed noodles, fish *en papillote,* and on the Sunday picnic, elk, antelope, or deer meat. Children will appreciate the hamburgers.

Circle Bar capably fulfills kids' needs and desires even without the services of a full-time counselor. Among her many talents, Sarah recorded two albums of children's songs and "lost a Grammy Award to Kermit the Frog in 1977." Her son Peter and daughter Melissa and Rick's two children keep the ball rolling as well, especially if it's in the pool for a mean volleyball game.

Children will also want to help milk the cow, feed the kittens, or gather eggs. Many events happen spontaneously, as when a group of teenagers coerced Sarah's assistant into decorating the hayloft for a night of western swing, complete with piñatas of a circle and a bar, which the smaller children made and filled with candy, handwritten fortunes, and toys. The scheduled activities follow more established lines: a hayride, cookouts, and fishing.

The weather in the valley tends to be warmer than in the Rockies, so the pool, kept at a constant 86 degrees, is a welcome diversion. An inviting hot tub also attracts guests on the occasional cool day or following a strenuous ride.

AVERILL'S FLATHEAD LAKE LODGE GUEST RANCH

BIGFORK, MONTANA

An exciting mix of land and lake activities

FLATHEAD Lake Lodge Dude Ranch more closely resembles a first-class country club than a typical dude ranch. Well-manicured grounds stretch down to a thirty-mile-long, nine-mile-wide crystal clear lake, where swimsuit-clad guests bask in the sun while others vie for time on the waterskis and Ski-Bob.

Nestled between Glacier National Park and the nation's largest wilderness area, the ranch offers many scenic wonders on horseback. There are more scenic experiences in the Jewel Basin primitive area, but there it is hiking on foot only.

The lodge's unique program of water activities augments their more traditional ranch activities. "We hire ranch kids, preferably with a rodeo background," co-owner/manager Doug Averill says of his

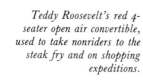

BOVE and LEFT. Some
ests choose days by the
ol and nights by the camp
e, while others sail and
de.

Teddy Roosevelt's red 4-
seater open air convertible,
used to take nonriders to the
steak fry and on shopping
expeditions.

wranglers. In 1987 they had on staff the Montana state rodeo queen and a professional with a background in outdoor recreation. Add to that the numerous students who work here for college credits in hotel management, nutrition, marketing, or outdoor recreation, and you can see why Doug takes pride in his staff.

Buck, the corral boss who has worked at the lodge for six summers, is one of the few older staff members. He keeps the barn smelling so sweet that Doug holds the weekly dance there. Not to be confused with a square dance, this event centers around Rob Quist's live western and bluegrass music, which won top honors in the state in 1987.

When the barn's not used for strutting, it's a quiet place to observe the eight or so horses that are not part of the dude string. These beautiful animals take part in competitions and/or rodeo schools, a concept that the Averill family originated. Doug is well-qualified to help out. He and his partner, renowned cowboy artist Fred Fellows, won the Western Regional Team Roping Championship in 1977. At least once a week you'll be able to see Doug, the wranglers, and neighbors practicing during the steer-roping demonstration.

Riding through the highly wooded acreage by the lake affords wonderful views of the water in one direction and of the Swan Range in the other. At the beginning of the week rides can go out with as many as ten to a group. Within a few days, however, the number drops, sometimes to two or three, as guests participate in other ventures. Four Plexipave tennis courts, a heated pool set in

cowboy boot-shaped concrete, and an admirable assortment of tubing trips, river floats, pack trips, and fishing packages draws the crowd from the horses to the other activities. In addition, visitors can help themselves to canoes, fishing boats, and sailing sloops.

One guest moaned, "I can't decide." She also wanted to see Glacier National Park, a forty-five minute drive away, and the nearby Bison Range. Guests don't often leave the ranch, but some do to play golf, hike at Jewel Basin, go cherry picking, visit the local winery, or take in a play at the Bigfork Summer Theater.

The unique western hospitality lures many people to Flathead Lake Lodge, but it is the ranch's superb activities programming that brings them back again and again and again.

ABOVE. The bucking horse, tugged by ranch hands, is close enough to the real thing for most guests. RIGHT. The busy wranglers posed for a portrait, above, and the great hall of the log lodge, below.

RODEO

The rodeo is a popular event all summer.
Private ones, put on by individual ranches for their guests,
are like the one at Lost Valley Ranch, shown on the
opposite page. Well-known, prize winning public rodeos
like the one at Cody is shown below. Dates can be
checked because a schedule allows the cowboys
to go from one rodeo to another to compete.

ROPING

Russell True, of the White Stallion Ranch, demonstrates calf roping below at one of the private rodeos staged regularly at the ranch. The second rider entering the scene on the opposite page ropes the hind legs. Once the calf is down and held securely by the well-trained horses, it is ready for branding.

Ranch Information

ARIZONA

WHITE STALLION RANCH, 9251 W. Twin Peaks Rd., Tucson, AZ 85743; (602) 297-0252; Allen and Cynthia True, owners. **Open:** Oct. 1 through May 1. **Guest capacity:** 47. **Accommodations:** 25 adobe-style exterior and cabin units, plus 3 rooms in main ranch house; most with double bed and twin bed. Single cabins and suites available, some with small refrigerator. **Rates:** $82 to $98 per person per day, double occupancy; third person in room, $68 to $80; $105 to $108, single occupancy. No credit cards. Free pickup in Tucson. **Facilities:** Heated swimming pool, redwood hot tub therapy room, recreation room, tennis courts, exotic birds and petting zoo; laundry; store. No pets; boarding kennels in Tucson. **Activities:** Hayride, breakfast ride, Indian oven dinner, ranch rodeo and cutting horse demonstration, gymkhana, nature walk and shopping trip. Riding lessons for a modest extra charge. Most guests rent a car on Sunday and visit the Arizona-Sonora Desert Museum, Old Tucson, and Mission San Xavier del Bac. Golf nearby. **Elevation:** 2,300 feet. **Acreage:** 3,000; Saguaro National Monument West. **Directions:** From the Tucson airport, take I-10 to the Ina Rd. exit. Go under the freeway, taking a left onto Ina Rd. going west. At the first stop sign, turn right onto Silverbell Rd. Continue to road sign showing a Y; take the left fork over a hump and watch for signs.

LAZY K BAR RANCH, 8401 N. Scenic Dr., Tucson, AZ 85743; (602) 297-0702; Rosemary Blowitz and William Scott, owners; Carol Moore, manager. **Open:** Sept. 1 through June 30; minimum 3-day stay.

Guest capacity: 50. **Accommodations:** 23 rooms in one- to four-room cottages with air conditioning. **Rates:** $70 to $90 per day per person, double occupancy; $90 to $100, single. Third person in room, under 12, $15 per night; 12 to 17, $30; over 17, $60. Collect calls accepted. American Express, Diners Club, MasterCard, Visa accepted. Free pickup in Tucson. **Facilities:** Heated pool, outdoor hot tub, 2 lighted Laykold tennis courts, lighted volleyball court, shooting range, recreation hall; laundry; well-stocked store; no pets. **Activities:** Hayride, breakfast or lunch ride, ranch rodeos at Thanksgiving, Christmas, and Easter times, trap shooting ($20 per session), tennis lessons with pro ($20 per hour). Individual and group riding lessons for $15 and $10, respectively. Private and public golf courses nearby. Old Tucson, Arizona-Sonora Desert Museum, and Mission San Xavier del Bac nearby. **Elevation:** 2,300 feet. **Acreage:** 160; Saguaro National Monument West. **Directions:** From the Tucson airport, take I-10 to the Ina Rd. exit and turn left (west) onto Ina Rd. At the first stop sign, turn right onto Silverbell Rd. and continue for approximately 3 miles to Pima Farm Rd. Turn left; that road dead ends at the gate.

TANQUE VERDE RANCH, Route 8, Box 66, Tucson, AZ 85748; (602) 296-6275; Bob Cote, manager and owner. **Open:** All year. **Guest capacity:** 125. **Accommodations:** 59 spacious, modern rooms in main ranch house or cottage-casitas with individual heat/air control and telephone, some with fireplace and most with 2 queen size beds. **Rates:** $75 to $120, per day per person, double occupancy; $120 to $205, single. American Express, Visa, MasterCard accepted. Free pickup in Tucson with 4-night minimum stay. **Facilities:** Indoor and outdoor heated swimming pools, 2 saunas, Jacuzzi pool, exercise room with fitness equipment, 5 Laykold tennis courts; laundry; well-stocked gift shop; no pets. **Activities:** Counselor-supervised children's program in winter, unique bird banding program, nature hikes, breakfast rides, all-day rides, games on horseback, fishing in spring-fed lake, guided tours to

area sights for an additional fee (minimum requirements may apply). Golf privileges at two country clubs. **Pack trips:** additional $40 per person per day. **Elevation:** 2,800 feet. **Acreage:** 650; Saguaro National Monument East and Coronado National Forest. **Directions:** From Tucson take Speedway Blvd. east until it ends; bear left on the dirt ranch road.

GRAPEVINE CANYON RANCH, P.O. Box 302, Pearce, AZ 85625; (602) 826-3185; Eve and Gerry Searle, owners. **Open:** All year; spring and autumn roundups by reservation only. **Guest capacity:** 20; no children under 12. **Accommodations:** 10 cabins and cabin suites with heat and air conditioning, sundeck, and coffee pot. Suites have refrigerator and king-size bed. **Rates:** $80 per person per day, double occupancy for cabin suites; $60 for cabins; $80 to $100 per day, single occupancy. Horseback riding is $10 per hour. Unlimited riding is available as an option. MasterCard and Visa accepted. Pickup in Tucson is $50 per carload. **Facilities:** Solar-heated swimming pool open Apr. to Oct. No pets. No smoking in the dining room. **Activities:** All-day rides, moonlight rides, guided tours to mining camps, Mexico, Tombstone, and more (extra charge). Golf nearby. **Pack trips:** $160 per person first night and $80 each additional night. **Elevation:** 5,000 feet. **Acreage:** Part of a 30-section ranch; Dragoon Mountains National Forest. **Directions:** From Tucson take I-10 to exit 318 east of Benson, the Dragoon Rd. This road dead ends at Rt. 666. Turn right (south) and go to Sunsites. (Coming from the east, take exit 331 west of Willcox and go to Sunsites.) At the south end of Sunsites take Treasure Rd. to the west and follow signs to the ranch.

PRICE CANYON RANCH, P.O. Box 1065, Douglas, AZ 85607; (602) 558-2383; Alice and Scotty Anderson, owners. **Open:** All year; two-night minimum encouraged.

Guest capacity: 3 families (up to 5 per family) or 30 individuals in shared accommodations. **Accommodations:** 6 individual units including room in main ranch house with private bath and apartment with woodstove and kitchen, plus family bunkhouse with bath. **Rates:** $135 per couple per day; $75, single occupancy; sliding rates for parents and children. Small trailer park on ranch premises; ask for rates. No credit cards. Free pickup in Douglas; $80 each way per carload to and from Tucson. **Facilities:** Solar-heated spring-fed swimming pool open June to Sept., 3-day eventing course for English riding, 3-acre catfish pond with small boat. Pets are welcomed. **Activities:** ranch work, roundups, and brandings; lunch rides. **Pack trips:** additional $40 per person per day; hunting package available. **Elevation:** 5,600 feet. **Acreage:** 15,000; Coronado National Forest. **Directions:** From Tucson take I-10 east to Rte. 80 south; continue to Douglas, then north to mile marker 400. Watch for sign and take the marked left turn. The ranch is 7 miles down a dirt road with 3 gates.

COLORADO

SKYLINE GUEST RANCH, Box 67, Telluride, CO 81435; (303) 728-3757; Dave and Sherry Farny, owners. **Open:** June 1 to Oct. 7, Sunday-to-Sunday minimum; cabins open all year for skiers. **Guest capacity:** 35. **Accommodations:** 10 cozy rooms in the main lodge, suite in the annex; 5 cabins that sleep 2 to 8, with kitchen. **Rates:** $630 per person per week. European plan rates available in cabins. No credit cards. Free pickup at Telluride airport or bus station. **Facilities:** Sauna, wood-fired hot tub; stocked ponds; laundry; no pets; no smoking in the buildings. **Activities:** Lake swimming, fly-fishing instruction, jeep trips, mountaineering and hiking, Mesa Verde excursion, photography workshops (special rate), music festivals in town. **Pack Trips:** additional $25 per person per day. **Elevation:** 9,600 feet. **Acreage:** 180, San Juna Mountains. **Directions:** Ranch will send information on reservation.

WAUNITA HOT SPRINGS RANCH, 8008 County Road 887, Gunnison, CO 81230; (303) 641-1266; Rod and Junelle Pringle, owners. **Open:** May 31 to Sept. 26 for dude ranch activities; Dec. 15 to April 15 for winter activities; minimum stay of 6 days in high season. **Guest capacity:** 45. **Accommodations:** 26 rooms in the ranch house and main lodge. **Rates:** $525 per person per week, 16 years and older; sliding scale for children, from $265 to $495; call for information on discounts. No credit cards. Free pickup in Gunnison. **Facilities:** Small petting farm and recreation room on ranch; large hot-spring-fed swimming pool with water slide; stocked lakes; limited laundry; no pets. **Activities:** Supervised children's activities, four-wheel drive trips, overnight (bring sleeping bag), float trip, hayride, jamboree, square dancing, Arena Alympics. Black Canyon of the Gunnison nearby. Alcoholic beverages not allowed. **Elevation:** 8,946 feet. **Acreage:** 121 deeded, 400 leased; Gunnison National Forest. **Directions:** Take U.S. 50 19 mi. east of Gunnison to highway marker 176. Follow the sign and go north 8 mi. to the ranch.

LOST VALLEY RANCH, Route 2, Sedalia, CO 80135; (303) 647-2311; The Foster and Reynolds families, owners and managers. **Open:** Feb. through Nov., Sunday-to-Sunday minimum in summer; spring roundup and fall programs differ. **Guest capacity:** 100. **Accommodations:** 24 one- to three-bedroom cabins with fireplace. **Rates:** $775 per person per week; children 6 to 12, $675; children 3 to 5, $475. No credit cards. Pick up in Colorado Springs or Denver with 10 days' notice; $80 single, $125 per couple, $160 per family, round trip. **Facilities:** Heated swimming pool, trap shooting and target range (extra fee), whirlpool spas, 2 Plexipave tennis courts; laundry; well-stocked store; no pets. Will acknowledge requests for nonsmokers at assigned seating dinners. **Activities:** Children's program, staff melodrama and singing, staff rodeo, gymkhana, fishing. **Pack trips:** additional $30 per person. **Elevation:** 7,200 feet. **Acreage:** 800, 25,000 leased; Pike National Forest. **Directions:** From Denver take Colorado Rte. 285 west to Pine Junction and go south on Rte. 126 for 23 miles to Forest Service road 211; turn right for 9 miles to ranch.

LONGS PEAK INN AND GUEST RANCH, Longs Peak Route, Estes Park, CO 80517; (303) 586-2110; outside Colorado (800) 262-2034; Bob and Virginia Akins, owners. **Open:** early June to mid Sept., Sunday to Sunday stay encouraged; 2-night minimum. **Guest capacity:** 75. **Accommodations:** 29 one- and two-bath units, including 6 rooms in the lodge. **Rates:** $73 to $76 per person per day, double occupancy; $66 to $71, family rate for four; children's rates on sliding scale; single occupancy, add $23 per day. Weekly rates, from Sunday to Sunday only, offer about 10% savings from the daily rate. Reduced rates before July 10 and after Aug. 22. Plus horseback riding, additional $110 per week. Hourly and daily rates available. MasterCard and Visa accepted. Free pickup in Estes Park. Pickup in Denver, $85 per carload each way. **Facilities:** Heated pool, whirlbath bath, rec room, stocked ponds, tipis; small store area; full liquor license; no pets. **Activities:** Counselor-supervised children's program including an overnight campout (through Aug. 27), breakfast ride, wine-and-cheese ride, van tours to Estes Park and Rocky Mountain National Park, river rafting (extra fee), square dancing, bingo, nature talks, guided hikes, riding lessons (additional fee). Golf, tennis, aerial tramway nearby. **Overnight trail ride:** $50 per person additional without horse package; $15 with weekly horse package. **Elevation:** 8,956 feet. **Acreage:** 250; Roosevelt and Arapahoe national forests and Rocky Mountain National Park. **Directions:** Take Rte. 36 north from Denver through Boulder to Lyons. Turn onto Rte. 7 west (turning south) to the sign for Longs Peak Inn.

WIND RIVER RANCH

WIND RIVER RANCH, P.O. Box 3410, Estes Park, CO 80517; (303) 586-4212; the Irvin family, owners. **Open:** June to Sept.; 3-night minimum. **Guest capacity:** 55. **Accommodations:** 28 cabins and lodge rooms with individually controlled heat, 2 with stone fireplace. **Rates:** $84 to $92 per person per day, double occupancy; $105, single. $525 to $575 per person per week, double; $680, single. Children 2 to 13, $58 to $64 per day or $375 to $400 per week. Horseback riding, additional $110 per week; hourly and daily rates available. MasterCard, Visa, Choice accepted. Free pickup in Estes Park. **Facilities:** Swimming pool, outdoor whirlpool bath, stocked pond, rec hall. Beer and wine license for dining room. No pets. **Activities:** Counselor-supervised children's program, breakfast ride, river rafting (extra fee), bingo, nature talks. Golf, tennis, aerial tramway nearby. Many guests rent a car to tour Rocky Mountain National Park. **Elevation:** 9,200 feet. **Acreage:** 110; Roosevelt National Forest and Rocky Mountain National Park. **Directions:** From Denver take Rte. 36 north through Boulder and Lyons to Rte. 7 west 28 miles to the ranch. Watch for the sign on the right.

PEACEFUL VALLEY LODGE AND GUEST RANCH, Star Rte., Box 2811, Lyons, CO 80540; (303) 747-2881 and (303) 440-9632 from Denver; Karl and Mabel Boehm and Randy and Debbie Eubanks, owners. **Open:** All year; full dude ranch program from June through Aug; Sunday to Sunday stay encouraged; 6-day minimum. Less structured program in autumn; cross-country skiing in winter. **Guest capacity:** 120 in summer. **Accommodations:** 66 log cabins and hotel-style rooms, some with sundeck and balcony overlooking the river; others with whirlpool tub, refrigerator, and/or fireplace. **Rates:** $534 to $624 per person per 6-day week, double occupancy; $598.50 to $700 for 7-day week. Single occupancy $103.25 to $123 more. Sliding scale for children. Choice, Diners Club/Carte Blanche, MasterCard, Visa accepted. Pickup in Denver, $50 each way for up to 5 people, $10 per person thereafter. **Facilities:** Solar-heated indoor swimming pool, sauna, whirlpool bath, nursery room, stocked pond, tennis courts, rec room, children's petting farm, beautiful alpine-style chapel; laundry; well-stocked store; no pets. Liquor license. **Activities:** Counselor-supervised children's program (summer), teenage program, breakfast ride, all-day ride or van trip, gymkhana, Old West costume party, square dance parties, talent show, hayride, fishing in ponds and St. Vrain River; van tours of Rocky Mountain National Park, mining towns, etc.; golf nearby. **Pack trip:** Additional $30 per person; one-night only. Bring or rent sleeping bag and pad. **Elevation:** 8,474 feet. **Acreage:** 320; Roosevelt National Forest. **Directions:** From Denver take Rte. 36 north to Rte. 7 west to Rte. 72 south. The ranch is 4 miles west of the junction of Rtes. 7 and 72.

VISTA VERDE GUEST RANCH, P.O. Box 465, Steamboat Springs, CO 80477; (303) 879-3858; Frank and Winton Brophy, owners. **Open:** June 1 to end of Sept.; 3-day minimum stay, Sunday to Sunday stays in mid-summer. Hunting season in mid Oct. and cross-country skiing from mid Dec. through end of March. **Guest capacity:** 36. **Accommodations:** 8 charming log cabins with one- to three-bedrooms, kitchen, and porch. Fireplace in 6 cabins. **Rates:** $140 per person per day or $975 per person per week, including day whitewater rafting trip; sliding scale rates for children. No credit cards. Free pickup in Steamboat Springs and Hayden. **Facilities:** Indoor whirlpool bath, sauna, cold plunge, and exercise room; swimming hole; barnyard animals, playground, tipi, rec room; swimming pool and tennis nearby; no pets. **Activities:** Hot-air ballooning ($125 for adults, $110 for children), children's program, breakfast cookout, all-day ride, hayrides, gymkhana, Steamboat rodeo, whitewater rafting trip on the upper Colorado River, fishing, square dancing, guided backpack trips, gold-panning expeditions, kids' tipi overnight, musical evenings. Masseuse, $35 for 75 minutes. Fly fishing school, $45 per person for 3 people. Hot mineral springs, gondola ride, sailing, golf, and soaring (extra fee) on request. **Pack trip:** Two-day trip for up to four guests, $150 per person. **Elevation:** 7,800 feet. **Acreage:** 550; Routt National Forest and Mt. Zirkel Wilderness. **Directions:** Write to ranch for specifics and color brochure.

WYOMING

PARADISE GUEST RANCH, P.O. Box 790, Buffalo, WY 82834; (307) 684-7876; Jim and Leah Anderson, managers; Apache Oil Co., owner. **Open:** Memorial Day to Oct. 1; Sunday to Sunday minimum during peak season. **Guest capacity:** 65. **Accommodations:** 18 spacious deluxe renovated or new one- to three-bedroom cabins, all with fireplace, living room, kitchenette, and individual heating system. **Rates:** $675

to $725 per person per week, double occupancy; $725, single; $525 to 675 for three to six in a cabin; children 6 to 12, $525 to $575; 3 to 5, $350; 2 and under, $200. Off-peak weeks, 20% discount. MasterCard, Visa accepted. Free pickup in Sheridan; $30 per person per trip (3-person minimum) to and from Casper. **Facilities:** Heated swimming pool, whirlpool bath, rec room, French Creek Saloon with liquor license; tennis and golf nearby; laundry; store. No pets; kennel in Buffalo. **Activities:** Part-time counselor-supervised children's program, trout fishing (extra charge for instruction), breakfast and all-day rides, talent show, kids' overnight, kids' rodeo, square dance. **Pack trip:** 4-day trip into Frying Pan Lake base camp, $100 to $140 per person per day. **Elevation:** 7,600 feet. **Acreage:** 158; Big Horn National Forest. **Directions:** From Buffalo drive 13 miles west on Rte. 16; watch for the brown U.S. Forest Service sign and turn right on Hunter Creek Rd. Follow the signs to the ranch.

SPEAR-O-WIGWAM RANCH, Box 1081, Sheridan, WY 82801-1081; (307) 674-4496; Jim and Barbara Niner, managers; Jack and Doris Riehm, owners. **Open:** June 15 to Sept. 15; 3-day minimum encouraged. Autumn hunting season, oct. and Nov.; cross-country skiing Jan. through March. **Guest capacity:** 30. **Accommodations:** 7 one- to four-bedroom cabins. **Rates:** $85 per person per day or $550 per week; children 7 through 12, $60 per day or $375 per week; children 2 through 6, $35 per day, $225 per week. Off-peak discounts. No credit cards. Free pickup in Sheridan; $50 round-trip pickup in Billings, MT. **Facilities:** stocked pond for children, rec room; beer license for dining room; pets okay but call to confirm. **Activities:** Picnic ride, lake swimming, excursion to Bradford Brinton Memorial and polo in Bighorn, musical evening; guests often go to the rodeos and horse shows in Buffalo and Sheridan. **Pack trips:** Trips into base camp just outside of the Cloud Peak Wilderness Area; additional $15 per person per day. **Elevation:** 8,300 feet. **Acreage:** 17; surrounded on all sides by Big Horn National Forest. **Directions:** From I-90 north (east), take Rte. 335 through Big Horn (blacktop and gravel road). Continue up the mountain and watch for signs. From the west, take U.S. Forest Service Rd. 631 (gravel) off Rte. 14, 5 miles south of Burgess Junction.

CASTLE ROCK CENTRE

CASTLE ROCK CENTRE, 412 County Rd. 6NS, Cody, WY 82414; (307) 587-2076 or (307) 527-7159; the Wieters family, owners; Bill and Robin Wieters Sprague, managing hosts. **Open:** Memorial Day through Sept., 3-day minimum stay. Other programs available year-round. **Guest capacity:** 32. **Accommodations:** 9 one- to two-bedroom units in cabins that sleep from one to six, some with fireplace and views of the Shoshone River. **Rates:** $95 to $115 per person per day; $575 to $725 per person per week, double occupancy, each additional occupant, $505 to $560. Rates are all-inclusive. Advance reservation rate discount. No credit cards. Pickup at Cody airport (no extra charge). **Facilities:** Heated pool, sauna, toy corner, rec room; laundry; infirmary with resident R.N.; no pets; no smoking in the dining room. **Activities:** Counselor-supervised children's program, breakfast ride, all-day ride, ranch rodeo, mountain climbing instruction, kayaking instruction, rafting, archery, mountain biking, sailing and windsurfing on the Cody Reservoir, power boat for interpretive trips and fishing, visits to Buffalo Bill Historical Center and Cody Nite Rodeo, interpretive trip to Yellowstone National Park, crafts center. **Pack trips:** by horseback. Llama treks also available. **Elevation:** 5,600 feet Acreage: 330; Absaroka Mountains. **Directions:** Write to ranch for specifics.

GRIZZLY RANCH. North Fork Rte., Cody, WY 82414; (307) 587-3966; Rick Felts, owner. **Open:** June 1 through Labor Day, 3-day minimum stay. Other seasonal programs available. **Guest capacity:** 15. **Accommodations:** 4 simple cabins sleeping from 2 to 6 people. **Rates:** $490 per person for a 7-day stay (Sunday to Sunday preferred); $390 for a 5-day stay; $290 for a 3-day stay. Children's rates range from

$70 for child 4 to 6 for 3-day stay to $390 for child 6 to 12 for the 7-day stay. No charge for children under 4. Discounts available. No credit cards. Free pickup in Cody. Pickup in Billings, $100 per group per trip (one way). **Facilities:** Stocked pond; tennis courts and golf course in town; ask Rick about bringing pets. **Activities:** River float and overnight pack trip (7-day stay only), tour of Yellowstone National Park and of Old Trial Town (5- and 7-day stay), visit to Buffalo Bill Historical Center, Cody Nite Rodeo; occasional ranch and cattle chores; all-day and breakfast rides. **Pack trips:** 4- and 7-day trips to a variety of destinations, $100 per person per day, minimum 3 people. **Elevation:** 6,000 feet. **Acreage:** 350; Shoshone National Forest. **Directions:** From Cody take Rte. 14/20 west 26 miles. Watch for the sign on the right.

ABSAROKA RANCH, Star Rte., Dubois, WY 82513; (307) 455-2275; Emi and Budd Betts, owners. **Open:** mid June through mid Sept.; hunting season in fall. **Guest capacity:** 16. **Accommodations:** 4 charming log cabins with one to two bedrooms and individual heating systems. **Rates:** $90 per person per day or $535 per week; children 12 and under, $75 per day or $445 per week. Children under 2 are free. Discounts for groups of 3 or more to a cabin and for repeat guests. No credit cards. Pickup in Riverton or Jackson, $75 for round trip. **Facilities:** Redwood sauna, recreation room; swimming pool and 9-hole golf course in town; no pets. **Activities:** All-day ride, game rides, square dances, rodeo in Riverton, Mountain Man talk, fishing, small boat for lake fishing, float trip (extra fee). Most guests take a day trip to Grand Teton and Yellowstone national parks. (Bring a flashlight.) **Pack trips:** Guided horseback and hiking pack trips available; write for separate brochure. **Elevation:** 8,000 feet. **Acreage:** Shoshone National Forest. **Directions:** On Rte. 26/287 go 10 miles west of Dubois (or 45 miles east of Grand Teton National Park). Signs will point the way 6 miles up the dirt Dunoir Valley Rd.

BITTERROOT RANCH, Rte. 66, Box 1042, Dubois, WY 82513; (307) 455-2778; outside Wyoming (800) 545-0019; Bayard and Mel Fox, owners. **Open:** June through Sept. **Guest capacity:** 30. **Accommodations:** 12 comfortable cabin units, most with woodburning stove and electric heat. **Rates:** $770 for the week. Single person supplement, $20 per day, July and Aug.; June and Sept., $10 per day. Children under 16, 25% off; under 4, $20 per day. No credit cards. Pickup in Riverton, $75 each way; in Jackson, $110 each way. **Facilities:** Two horses per guest, English and western tack, trout stream and stocked pond, pool room, peacocks, inflatable boat for children; Equitour horseback trips throughout the world; no pets; laundry. **Activities:** Jumping courses, videotaped lessons (occasionally), picnic rides, pony rides, fishing. **Pack trips:** Frequent trips, usually in small groups; additional $20 per person per day, 7 days or more total $100 per person per day. **Elevation:** 7,500 feet. **Acreage:** 630; Shoshone National Forest. **Directions:** Take Rte. 26 ten miles east of Dubois; turn north on East Fork Rd. the ranch is at the end of the road, 16 miles from Rte. 26.

LAZY L & B RANCH, Dubois, WY 82513; (307) 455-2839; Bernard and Leota Didier, owners. **Open:** middle May to Oct. 1; Sunday to Saturday minimum stay. **Guest capacity:** 30. **Accommodations:** 16 units ranging from a spacious two-story log cabin with kitchenette to single and double rooms with bath and shower. **Rates:** $490 per person per 6-day week; $325 for children under 12. No credit cards. Pickup in Jackson or Riverton, $80 per carload, round trip. **Facilities:** Solar heated pool, rec room, small lapidary shop, stocked pond; golf and tennis nearby; pets allowed but call first to confirm. **Activities:** Extensive riding on ranch and into the wilderness, fishing, breakfast rides on request, overnight at Upper Ranch, fishing, hayride, square dance, occasional corral games, limited children's program, daily happy hour. Guests may reserve a day to tour Yellowstone or the Tetons. **Elevation:** 7,200 to 8,500 feet. **Acreage:** 1,800; National Forest, Shoshone Indian Reservation, and State Elk Feeding Refuge. **Directions:** Take Rte. 26/287 ten miles east of Dubois. Turn north on East Fork Rd. Watch for sign to the ranch 12 miles north of Rte. 26/287.

TRAIL CREEK RANCH, Box 10, Wilson, WY 83014; (307) 733-2610; Elizabeth Woolsey, owner. **Open:** June 15 to Sept. 15; for skiers, Feb. and March. **Guest capacity:** 25. **Accommodations:** Comfortable bunkhouses, rooms, and cabins. **Rates:** (per person, per day) Bunkhouse, $75 per day; single rooms, $85 to $95; double rooms, $80 to $95; cabins, $80 to $95. No credit cards. Pickup in Jackson, modest charge. **Facilities:** Heated swimming pool, canoes, bumper pool table. **Activities:** Riding, gymkhanas, all-day trips, fishing, boating, pack trips. Write directly to ranch for information. **Elevation:** 6,280 feet. **Acreage:** 320; Teton National Forest. **Directions:** Take Rte. 22 through Wilson. One mile outside of town watch for the Heidelberg Inn; take a left on the road across from the inn (you'll see a small sign). The ranch is on the left.

HEART SIX RANCH, P.O. Box 70, Moran, WY 83013; (307) 543-2477; the Garnick family, owners. **Open:** June 1 to Sept. 15; minimum Sunday to Sunday stay. Hunting and hiking season in fall. **Guest capacity:** 55. **Accommodations:** 11 one- to three-room units, some with wood-burning stove/fireplace. **Rates:** $575 to $700 per person per week, double occupancy; $595 to $625, single; $575 to $650 for more than two in a room. Children 3 to 6, half price; under 2, free. American Express, Discover, MasterCard, Visa accepted. Free pickup in Jackson or Jackson Hole airport. **Facilities:** Heated swimming pool, canoes, rec room, Sanen goats; smoking in lodge in Beaver Slide Saloon only; laundry in ranch store; no pets. **Activities:** All-day and breakfast rides, hayrides, square dance, theater in Jackson, Mountain Man or Indian dancing demonstration, kids overnight in tipi village, nature walk, moonlight ride, Jackson rodeo, fishing, float trips ($10 to $22.50 per person), canoe rental ($14 or $27, half or full day), guided full-day float, horseback, or walk-in fishing trips (extra charge), children on lead horse ($10 per hour); van to Jenny Lake and other sights (extra fee). **Pack trips:** Write directly to ranch for information. **Elevation:** 7,200 feet. **Acreage:** 2,000; Teton Wilderness. **Directions:** Write to ranch for specifics.

MONTANA

LAZY K BAR RANCH, Box 550, Big Timber, MT 59011; (406) 537-4404; the Van Cleve family, owners. **Open:** June 23 through Labor Day, 7-day minimum. Reservations are essential; no "drop-in" guests are accepted. References required. **Guest capacity:** 45. **Accommodations:** 22 charming one- to four-bedroom cabins, some with living room, fireplace, or Franklin stove; a few without bath. **Rates:** $400 to $600 per person per week depending on type and size of cabin and degree of occupancy. Children under 6, fifty percent less; ages 1 to 3, no charge. No credit cards. Pickup in Billings or Bozeman, $90 per trip each way. **Facilities:** Solar-heated swimming pool, billiards table; extensive and unusual library; laundry service or coin operated launderette; well-stocked store; no pets. On request, a no-smoking area in the dining room will be designated. **Activities:** Unlimited riding, occasional cattle ranch chores, all-day rides, wrangler-supervised children's activities, moonlight ride, breakfast walk, fishing, square dance, occasional talent show; tours to Yellowstone National Park, ghost towns, Hutterite colony, etc. (extra fee). **Elevation:** 6,000 feet. **Acreage:** 26,000 acres, some of which is intermingled with Gallatin National Forest. **Directions:** The ranch is about 14 miles from the blacktop. Call ranch for directions.

Cattle Brand **Horse Brand**

63 RANCH, P.O. Box 979, Livingston, MT 59047; (406) 222-0570; Virginia Christensen and Sandra and Bud Cahill, owners. **Open:** Mid June to mid Sept.; hunting season, Sept. and Oct.; winter cabin available. **Guest capacity:** 30. **Accommodations:** 8 cabins with one- to four-rooms and electric, propane, or woodstove heat. **Rates:** $75 per person per day or $425 to $495 per week; subtract $15 per week for children 11 and under. (Rates may vary.) No credit cards. Pickup in Bozeman, $35 per carload each way; in Billings, $65. **Facilities:** Swimming hole, stocked pond, rec room. Well-behaved pets okay. **Activities:** Occasional cattle ranch chores, all-day rides, wagonrides, *tipi* overnight for children, square dance. Most guests visit the museum in Livingston, an offshoot of the Buffalo Bill Historical Center in Cody. **Pack trips:** Additional $45 per person per day; 3-day minimum. **Elevation:** 5,600 feet. **Acreage:** 1,900; Gallatin National Forest. **Directions:** Write to ranch for specifics.

NINE QUARTER CIRCLE RANCH, Canyon Rte., Gallatin Gateway, MT 59730; (406) 995-4276; Kim and Kelly Kelsey, owners. **Open:** Mid June to mid Sept., one-week minimum stay; hunting season, late Oct. to late Nov. **Guest capacity:** 80. **Accommodations:** 23 one- to four-bedroom cabins, some with wood-burning stove or fireplace. **Rates:** $525 per person per week, double occupancy; $567, single; sliding scale for children. Off-peak and extended stay discounts. No credit cards. Pickup in Bozeman, $17.50 per person, round trip; in West Yellowstone, $15. **Facilities:** Airstrip, "glorified swimming hole," playground, stocked pond; laundry; store; no pets. **Activities:** Counselor-supervised children's program, all-day rides, square dance, gymkhana, overnight pack trip (bring sleeping bag), daily happy hour, Ennis rodeo in June, fishing. **Pack trips:** Extended pack trips are available for an additional $35 per person per day. **Elevation:** 7,000 feet. **Acreage:** 440; Gallatin National Forest. **Directions:** Take I-90 to Bozeman, then Rte. 191 south 58 miles. Turn right on Taylors Fork; follow signs 5 miles to the ranch. From the south, go through West Yellowstone on Rte. 191 north, drive 33 miles, then turn left on Taylors Fork and watch for signs.

LONE MOUNTAIN RANCH, P.O. Box 69, Big Sky, MT 59716; (406) 995-4644; Michael H. Ankeny and Bob and Viv Schaap, owners. **Open:** Mid June to mid Oct., minimum one-week stay encouraged, Sunday arrival recommended; cross-country ski season, Dec. 6 to April 16. **Guest capacity:** 50. **Accommodations:** 20 comfortable cabins with electric heat and fireplace or wood-burning stove. **Rates:** $680 per person per week, double occupancy; $850, single; $520 to $660 for three to nine people in cabin. Children's rates on sliding scale. Off-season and extended stay discounts. American Express, MasterCard, Visa accepted. Free pickup in Bozeman and West Yellowstone. **Facilities:** Whirlpool bath, playground, pool room; Horsefly Saloon with full liquor license; Orvis-endorsed store; golf, tennis, and heated pool nearby; laundry. No pets. No smoking in the dining room. **Activities:** Counselor-supervised children's program, Orvis-endorsed fly-fishing program, all-day rides and guided hikes, tipi overnight for children, wine-and-cheese ride, nature walks, birdwatching walks, orienteering workshop, campfires, ranch rodeo, fly-casting clinic, tours of Yellowstone National Park—tourist sights and backcountry (extra fee), whitewater rafting (extra fee), off-ranch riding (extra fee), guided fishing trips (extra fee). Cross-country ski packages and cooking seminars also available. Climbing school nearby. **Pack trips:** $105 to $125 per person per day. Guided fishing trips by horseback also available. **Elevation:** 6,500 feet. **Acreage:** 2,000; Spanish Peaks Primitive Area. **Directions:** Write to ranch for specifics.

DIAMOND J RANCH, Box 577, Ennis, MT 59729; (406) 682-4867; Peter and Jinny Combs, owners. **Open:** First week in June through Sept., Sunday to Sunday minimum. **Guest capacity:** 35. **Accommodations:** 10 log cabins with stone fireplace, gas heater, and hickory furniture. **Rates:** (1988 rates) $700 per person per week: $350, children 12 and under.

MasterCard accepted. Pickup in Bozeman, $35 each way. **Facilities:** An Orvis-endorsed ranch. Heated pool, one indoor cement tennis court; no smoking in the dining room; no pets. **Activities:** Occasional cattle ranch chores (on separate ranch in the Madison Valley), breakfast ride or square dance, skeet and trap shooting (extra fee), fishing, daily happy hour, float trip (extra fee). Most guests rent a car to visit Virginia City and Nevada City. **Pack trips:** Additional $25 per person per day. **Elevation:** 5,800 feet. **Acreage:** 300; Beaverhead National Forest. **Directions:** Seventy miles north of Yellowstone National Park; write to ranch for specifics.

BEARTOOTH RANCH, Route 2, Box 350, Nye, MT 59061; (406) 328-6194 and 328-6205; Jim and Ellen Langston, managers. **Open:** June 1 to Labor Day; no minimum, but Sunday arrival strongly recommended; limited hunting season in fall. **Guest capacity:** 30. **Accommodations:** 11 motel-like rooms in Woodbine Lodge; 9 log or log-and-fieldstone guest cabins, some with fireplace or woodstove. **Rates:** (1988 rates) $60 per person per day, double occupancy, or $420 per week; single occupancy, 20% more. Children under 4 free. No credit cards. Pickup in Billings, $60 for the round trip. **Facilities:** Swimming hole, recreation lodge; laundry; pets discouraged. **Activities:** Trout fishing, children's program, bonfire, all-day ride, picnic ride, square dancing, treasure hunt. **Pack trips:** July 15 to September 25; write for rates. **Elevation:** 5,058 feet. **Acreage:** 1,000; Absaroka-Beartooth Wilderness Area. **Directions:** Write to ranch for specifics.

CIRCLE BAR GUEST RANCH, Utica, MT 59452; (406) 423-5454; Sarah Hollatz, owner. **Open:** June to Sept., 3-day minimum; hunting season, Sept. and Oct.; winter season stays available. **Guest capacity:** 45. **Accommodations:** 7 one- to four-bedroom log cabins with individual

heat systems, wet bar, and living area; some with fireplace. Plus one ski-lodge style room in ranch house. **Rates:** $630 per person per week; $420, children 12 and under. No credit cards. Pickup in Great Falls, $100 round trip; in Lewistown, $50 round trip. **Facilities:** Heated pool, whirlpool bath, playground, rec room, farm animals; call to confirm about pet policy; laundry. **Activities:** Occasional cattle ranch chores, all-day and moonlight rides, hayride, square dance, gymkhana, local rodeo, fishing, four-wheel drive trips; Charlie Russell's cabin reconstruction, Utica Museum, and Yogo Mine Visitor's Center nearby. **Pack trips:** Additional $20 per person per day. **Elevation:** 5,200 feet. **Acreage:** 2,500; Lewis and Clark National Forest and the Judith River State Elk Preserve. **Directions:** Write to ranch for specifics.

AVERILL'S FLATHEAD LAKE LODGE DUDE RANCH, Box 248, Bigfork, MT 59911-0248; (406) 837-4391; Doug and Maureen Averill, owner-managers. **Open:** May through Sept., Sunday to Sunday minimum; roundup week in Sept. **Guest capacity:** 110. **Accommodations:** 19 comfortable rooms in lodge primarily for singles and couples, plus 17 charming two- to three-bedroom cottages with individual heat systems. **Rates:** $875 per person per week, double occupancy; single, $980; children on a sliding scale: teens, $693, 4 to 12, $595, under 4, $96. No credit cards. Pickup in Kalispell or Whitefish, $20 round trip. **Facilities:** Heated swimming pool, 4 Plexipave tennis courts, rec room, 50-foot racing sloop, canoes, sailboats, motorboats; golf course nearby; laundry; no pets. Bring your own beach towels. **Activities:** Counselor-supervised children's activities, children's tipi overnight (bring sleeping bag), breakfast ride, beach fires, barn dance, ranch rodeo and gymkhana, roping demonstrations, fly-fishing instruction, boating, sailing instruction, windsurfing, waterskiing, lake cruises; river tubing, whitewater and flatwater river floats, fly-in fishing trips, canoeing trips (extra fees); daily happy hour. Many guests rent a car to visit Glacier National Park, Jewel Basin Primitive Area for hiking, National Bison Range, and Bigfork Summer Theater. **Pack trips:** Approximately $50 additional fee per person per day. **Elevation:** 3,000 feet. **Acreage:** 2,000. **Directions:** Write to ranch for specifics.

Bitterroot Ranch, Wyoming